The Brilliance Breakthrough

How To Talk And Write So That People Will Never Forget You

Eugene M. Schwartz

Foreword

This masterpiece you now hold in your hands, which has been a lost classic from almost the day Gene Schwartz wrote it, might be the most influential book you will ever read assuming you plan on communicating with other human beings in the future.

It is for me... and it has taught me more about communicating verbally and through the written word than anything I learned in my four years of college as an English major.

Back story on that: When I returned home from my sophomore year of college and told my parents I would be majoring in English, I came dangerously close to being cut off from my "college funding"; and even worse, I thought my parents would kick me out of the house.

But things worked out (or so I thought).

I was able to graduate with a degree in English and I believed that by sticking to my guns and not changing my major (and convincing my parents I would use my English degree for good rather than evil), I learned how to read and write and I was destined for greatness.

But everything changed when I got to know (and learn from) Gene Schwartz just a few years after graduating from college.

This book will forever change the way you think, and have been taught, about expressing yourself and your ideas.

And while I don't want to make it seem like "copywriting is easy," *The Brilliance Breakthrough* is the next best thing to having Gene Schwartz as your personal writing coach. This book is not a magic bullet but it will significantly increase your chances of becoming a much more effective writer and communicator.

As a first step, Gene makes it perfectly clear what you need to know about this book with the opening sentence of Chapter 1:

"The first thing you have to do with this book is forget everything you were ever taught about grammar!"

Gene's thesis (and subtitle of the book) of teaching us, "How To Talk And Write So That People Will Never Forget You" has less to do with grammar and "proper English" and more to do with choosing the perfect words to make up the sentences we speak and write for maximum impact.

And yes, this is a marketing book at its core so "maximum impact" means "maximum sales."

Why have I been obsessed about bringing The Brilliance Breakthrough back to life?

I think the main reason is that everyone practicing copywriting or marketing today needs as much Gene Schwartz in their life as possible.

I believe he might be the most important figure in the history of advertising when it comes to the merging of human behavior with copywriting and marketing.

And since I like to say, "marketing isn't everything, it's the only thing" (in the context of how to get your mission or vision out to as many people as possible and as powerfully as possible), learning how to write like Gene (which you will from this book) is your ticket to creating the most powerful messaging possible.

As Gene says at the conclusion of chapter three:

"...from words, you have generated images. And now from these images you will generate sentences. And from these sentences you will then generate entire discourses. Stories, reports, instructions, poems... a universe of shared emotions and thoughts."

Despite the fact that Gene never wrote anything for an online promotion, what he is talking about here – and throughout the book – applies to all media and forms of communication: Sales letters, space ads, email, video scripts etc. – any written communication that has as its main purpose to get the reader to respond... and buy.

Online or offline.

I think you will also be struck by how simple Gene's writing approach seems to be and his willingness to peel back the curtain on that approach... word by word, sentence by sentence.

The exercises at the end of each chapter – almost like "Mad Libs" for copywriting (but way more productive and with "correct answers" in the book!) – will guide you through a process that will make you a better writer.

Also, please follow Gene's instructions on how to use this book best.

He emphasizes the importance of applying the lessons from each chapter *immediately.* So if you can, please attack the book as Gene recommends… you won't be disappointed.

And since I was always taught to never write inside the pages of a book (until I got to college!) – especially one as valuable as this one – I wanted to make it as easy as possible for you to apply Gene's techniques.

That's why I created the accompanying workbook which includes all of the exercises which appear at the end of each chapter.

The workbook will also make it easier to toggle between the book and the exercises in the workbook.

These exercises will enable you to write in ways you never thought possible.

I firmly believe that when you are working inside your passion – when your work is truly your play – you can become the best copywriter for your business.

That's not to say that if you ever have an opportunity to hire a copywriter of Gene Schwartz's caliber you shouldn't jump at that opportunity – but most of us will not be given that opportunity in our lifetime.

However, this book, and the process Gene lays out for us step-by-step, is the best way for you to bring out what is inside of you… enable you to write incredibly powerful copy… with the possibility of needing only a proofreader when you are done.

And remember… the proofreading will have little to do with proper grammar.

So that's why this book needs to be brought back to life… and it is no accident why the price of used copies of this book have been offered online for as much as $8,000…and as of this printing, the cheapest used copy I've seen is around $4,000.

Only a select few have been able to apply *The Brilliance Breakthrough*... until now.

What makes this book different from Gene's other masterpiece, Breakthrough Advertising?

If you think *The Brilliance Breakthrough* is *Breakthrough Advertising II: The Sequel,* think again. It's a very different kind of book.

But that does not diminish its importance and how it relates to Gene's more well known volume.

In a perfect world, I would have preferred re-publishing *The Brilliance Breakthrough* before *Breakthrough Advertising* since this book, while not a primer for copywriters, is not nearly as dense as *Breakthrough Advertising* – and it is immediately usable and practical to many more people.

I think if you read *The Brilliance Breakthrough* first, you will get more hands-on training before diving into what is clearly Gene's "advanced course" (i.e. *Breakthrough Advertising*).

But no biggie if you have already read *Breakthrough Advertising* and you are now beginning to read this treasure.

I would highly recommend, however, that you re-read *Breakthrough Advertising* after you have been through *The Brilliance Breakthrough.*

The fact is that neither of these books can be read just once to garner their full impact anyway.

In short, *The Brilliance Breakthrough* is all about execution on the theories Gene Schwartz penned as copywriting rules of thumb (and universals about human behavior) in *Breakthrough Advertising.*

You need *both* of these books in your library... they complement each other beautifully... and this is the first time in decades that both are easily accessible to all generations of marketers and copywriters.

How lucky are you to have easy access to The Brilliance Breakthrough?

Well... luckier than when I was a lad.

The stories I have heard over the years about smuggling

copies of this book out of libraries are legendary.

Publisher and direct marketing historian (and my partner in getting this new edition printed), Jim DiCola, told me this story:

I went to my library [many years ago] and requested an interlibrary loan. After checking across the country, the only copy they could find was from the Library of Congress.

A month later the book showed up at my local branch.

However they had strict instructions that they would not let the book leave the library due to restrictions from the Library of Congress and that it was only on loan for a short period of time.

So every Saturday morning (and some weekday evenings) I would trek a mile to my local library, go to the front desk and request the book, and then a staff member would have to personally go to some secure part of some back room and bring me the book to read on the premises only.

And as the due date approached for when they had to return the book to the Library of Congress, I had been successful in my secret mission to photocopy the entire book, one chapter at a time, unbeknownst to them.

And Brian, I will not tell you where this library is located… ever!

Of course I asked Jim if I could make the story richer by saying he walked 12 miles each way to the library, in the snow, and barefoot as well… however, what he told me above was the best he could do.

But you get the idea.

I've heard other stories from folks who had to leave significant "collateral" at the front desk at their library in order to read *The Brilliance Breakthrough* on site.

I was frantically looking for someone who might have forfeited their Rolex to sneak out of their library with the book… hey $4,000 could buy a pretty nice watch, right?

Sadly, I couldn't get that story and decided not to make one up.

But the good news is that the book is no longer rare.

And congratulations that you now own a copy.

Are you ready to become your own best copywriter?

I want to thank Gene for being such an incredible mentor to me and so many others during his lifetime.

And I also want to thank his wonderful wife, Barbara Schwartz, for being so generous with Gene while he was with us... and to this day.

Her generosity is the main reason this book is now available to you.

When I approached her about re-publishing this book, she only had one copy of the original text herself... which I have not let out of my sight while using it to print this new version.

Yes... I did a little photocopying myself.

I also made a very cool discovery while going through Barbara's copy which was clearly a message from Gene to me (and to you): There were actually notes from Gene inside Barbara's copy with changes he wanted to make to some of the chapter titles should the book ever be reprinted.

Of course all of those changes have been incorporated into this edition.

And seeing those notes made it abundantly clear that Gene also wants to be part of getting this book back into circulation... and to share his wisdom with all of you.

Like Barbara, Gene was very generous too... and I am so gratified seeing the appetite for Gene's work today, even among the youngest copywriters and marketers... but I am also not surprised.

And this book in particular, while on the surface looks like it is targeted at copywriters and marketers, is really for anyone who desires to speak or write more clearly.

I know of quite a few people who want to give it to their children... one friend is buying a copy for his 11 year old son.

I know Gene is smiling down on all of us, seeing the impact his work has had on multiple generations already... and also how much more impact he will be making on generations into the future.

It's obvious that Gene practiced what he preached:

He knew better than anyone how to talk and write so that people will never forget him.

Brian Kurtz
May 2017

CONTENTS

PART ONE

PART TWO

HOW TO MAKE
WHAT YOU SAY OR WRITE
UNFORGETTABLE!

PART ONE

Chapter 1

The Two Main
Parts of Grammar

THE FIRST THING you have to do with this book is forget everything you were ever taught about grammar!

If you were taught grammar in school, your ability to speak well, and write well, was crippled. Because the old grammar – the school grammar – is not only wrong, but disastrous. And you simply have to forget all of it now.

First of all, you have to throw away its definitions. You have to realize that there are no such things as nouns, pronouns, verbs, adjectives, and all the rest. (They never did make sense, did they?)

Forget even their names. No more nouns. No more pronouns. No more verbs. None of them work. None of them show you how to take your thoughts, put them into words, and link the words together into sentences that are simple, that are clear, and that make other people think the way you do.

Here, instead, are some definitions, and rules, that do just that.

We can say, as our first rule, that all language is made up of two – and just two – working parts. Two different kinds of words.

The first of these is what we will call *Picture Words*. (Or, if you wish, *Image Words.*)

And the second is what we will call *Connecting Words*. (Or, if you wish, *Relation Words.*)

These are our two main parts – the only two elements that we will use to construct our flow of sentences. They replace all the old useless parts. And they do things for you that nouns, verbs, adjectives, etc. could never dream of doing.

Here are their definitions:

A *Picture Word* is a *word that carries a built-in picture within it.*

When you say a Picture Word by itself, you see or hear or feel or imagine something. Like *Rose. Tree. Boy. Harry. Hit. Itch. Thump. Blue. Swim. Slowly. Explosion. Truth.* And all the rest.

Each one of these words carries a picture inside itself. That picture stands out by itself. You need no other words to support it. It is there. It exists. You can see it. Smell it. Taste it. Touch it. Draw it. Show it on movie film.

And, above all, you can be sure when you say it that the other person sees just about the same picture, too.

Now, when we want to tell other people our thoughts, we can use several different kinds of Picture Words. Here are some of them:

There are Picture Words that show us things. *Ship. World. Betty. Julius Caesar. Rifle. Forest. Road. New York City.* And all the rest.

There are Picture Words that show us *actions. Hit. Sleep. Run. Argue. Make. Transfer. Procrastinate.* And all the rest.

There are Picture Words that show us *colors. Red. Green. Orange. Lavender. Fuchsia.* And all the rest.

There are Picture Words that show us *size. Tall. Fat. Long. Microscopic. Gargantuan.* And all the rest.

There are Picture Words that show us *details* of other pictures. *Torn. Embroidered. Tearful. Slowly. Laughingly.* And all the rest.

There are Picture Words that show us *feelings. Joy. Hate. Love. Lust.* And all the rest.

There are Picture Words that show us *judgments. Bad. Good. Right. Wrong. Interesting. Dull.*

There are Picture Words that show us *ideas. Truth. Justice. Liberty. Democracy. Parameter. Id. Ego. Antidisestablishmentarianism.* And all the rest.

And – as the most powerful tool of all – there are Picture Words that show us *more than one kind of picture,* depending on how they are used in a sentence.

For example, the Picture Word *sail* can give you more than one picture. If you say, "Hoist the *sail,"* you see one thing. But if you say, "I'm going out to *sail* my boat," you see an entirely different picture.

As you'll see, it's "slippery" words like *sail* – that shift their meanings according to how you place them in your sentences – that give you the tools you need to build punch, charm, and humor into your sentences.

There are, then, all kinds of Picture Words. But the kinds (or categories) of them are not important. What is important is their definition – *that every one of them carries its own built-in picture.* And that they help you transfer that picture from your mind to the mind of someone else.

Once again, every time you say one of them, you see something. And the person you're talking to also sees that same something.

Therefore, they are different from our second kind of word ... the *Connecting Word.*

A Connecting word has no built-in picture within it.

When you say a Connecting Word by itself, therefore, you don't see anything. Like *a ... the ... in ... over ... and ... yet ... to ... when ... before.*

And especially *is ... was ... be.* And all the rest.

Try them. Unless you put them in a sentence, they give you no picture at all.

If you say them by themselves, they automatically seem incomplete.

You automatically say, *"a* what?" ... *"the* what?" ... *"and* what?" ... *"over* what?" ... *"to* what?" ... *"is* what?"

By themselves, they are incomplete. They mean something only when they are joined to another word – a Picture Word.

What, then, is their use? Very simple. They tell us how the Picture Words go together.

They tell us how the Picture Words are *connected* to each other. In time. In space. In meaning. And in sequence.

They put the Picture Words in their correct places. They sort the Picture Words out for us.

They arrange them in logical order – with sentences, and between sentences.

That's why we call them Connecting Words. A *Connecting Word is a word that shows us the connection between our Picture Words.*

Picture Words alone don't do this. To use a classic example, take the Picture Words "Ship sails tomorrow."

This is ambiguous; it can mean two things. And it needs an almost-invisible Connecting Word, *"the,"* to sort out these two meanings.

Put the *"the"* in one place, and you have: "The ship sails tomorrow." But put it in another place between the same Picture Words, and you have: "Ship the sails tomorrow."

Therefore, to get our meaning precise – to avoid confusion when we talk to someone – we need both kinds of words.

We need *Picture Words.* And we need *Connecting Words.*

We have to point things out. And we have to show how they fit together. How they connect, or relate, to each other.

And *grammar* is *the way we put these two kinds of words together, to make our meanings precise.*

This is all of the new grammar in a nutshell. We take two kinds of words. We learn the best ways to put them together. And then we use them to tell other people our thoughts.

Everything else follows from this simple procedure. The rest of this book is just about how we do this. About how we take these two building blocks – these two kinds of words – and use them to write novels, and poetry, and textbooks, and business reports. Or sing songs. Or speak out at a business conference or a town meeting. Or gossip over a fence. Or whisper marvelous little lies into a soft and willing ear.

Here is how we start ...

A SPECIAL NOTE

You have now finished Chapter 1. In it, you have learned certain definitions, and the rules that put them to work.

I assume, however, that you will want more practice immediately in proving that they do work. Therefore, I have put some exercises and applications of these rules at the end of each chapter.

I would suggest that you turn to them now, and do the exercises and applications given there for Chapter 1.

Then go on to Chapter 2. And go through the remaining chapters of the book in the same way.

The answers to these exercises are given in each chapter of the book. If you have any questions, just go back and forth from exercise to the chapter.

Exercises and Applications

T HESE EXERCISES and Applications are to be done after you finish each one of the chapters.

They have a simple purpose: *To put into operation the terms and rules you have learned in each of these chapters.* To give you practice in:

Thinking with them.

Using them to solve problems.

And, above all, putting them to work – immediately – as tools to help you express your thoughts more effectively.

They are not, however, tests. They are not here to see whether you can repeat, like a parrot, the material given to you in each chapter.

This is exactly what you do not want to do. You do not want to repeat or memorize at all. Because then you would be using my thoughts instead of your own. And you would then have to come back to my answers to see whether you were right or wrong.

Then you would always be dependent on somebody else. And the whole purpose of education is to make you dependent on no one except yourself. To give you the proper tools – effective enough and logical enough – to do the thing right yourself, and know that you're right, without asking anyone else at all.

So what you do in these exercises is forget about repetition. And concentrate entirely on application. On using these rules so often – and proving that they work each time – that you become as comfortable with them as you are with your own name.

Exercises and Applications
for Chapter 1

For each exercise, either fill in the blank line or circle the correct word or phrase.

1.   There are only two definitions in this book that you really have to remember. The first of them is for a *Picture Word.* It is really quite simple. I'd like you to fill in the key word in it right now:

A Picture Word is a word that carries a built-in _____within it.

2.   There are all kinds of pictures, of course, that these Picture Words can show us. For example, there are Picture Words that show us *things.* In Chapter 1, I listed eight things that Picture Words can show us. There are thousands more. Would you list five more below:

_____

_____

3.   Some of the things Picture Words can show us are, of course, people. So please list five different Picture Word names of people here:

_____

_____

4.   Now list five new Picture Words that show us *actions:* (Make sure that at least two of them are action Picture Words that have more than one syllable each.)

_____

_____

5.   Now list five new Picture Words that show us *colors:*

_____

_____

6.   Now list five new Picture Words that show us *size:*

_____

_____

7.　Now list five new Picture Words that show us *details* of the things you have listed in 2 above.

_____

_____

8.　Now list five new Picture Words that show us *details of actions*. The actions you have listed in 4 above.

_____

_____

9.　Now list five new Picture Words that show us *details of people*. The people you have listed in 3 above.

_____

_____

10.　Now list five new Picture Words that show us *details of colors*. The colors you have listed in 5 above. (How about a *bright* blue - or a *yummy* yellow.)

_____

_____

11.　Now list five new Picture Words that show us *details of details* (like a *dazzlingly* bright blue – or a *surprisingly* tall boy):

_____

_____

12.　Now list five new Picture Words that show us *feelings:*

_____

_____

13.　Now list five new Picture Words that show us *judgments:*

_____

14.　Now list five new Picture Words that show us *ideas:*

_____

_____

15.   Would you say that Picture Words that show feelings could have other Picture Words with them that show details of these feelings? *(Yes/No)*.

16.   If your answer is Yes, then list five new Picture Words that show us the details of the feelings you have written in 12 above:

---

17.   Picture Words that show us details of judgments are very rare. We can say that something is *very* bad, or *completely* wrong, or *intolerably* dull. Can you list three more details of judgments here?

---

18.   And how about five new Picture Words that show us details of ideas:

---

19.   And now we come to those shifty words – the Picture Words that show more than one kind of picture, depending on how they are used in a sentence. For example, the word *blow*. It can give you one picture in a sentence like this:

"I struck him a hard *blow* to the chin."

Here it shows us a thing. Now write another sentence, using the same word, *blow,* but making it show us an action:

---

20.   Now write two sentences for the Picture Word *rock.* Make it show us a thing in the first sentence, and an action in the second:

---

21. Now write two sentences for the Picture Word *fast*. Make it show us a detail of an action in the first sentence, and an action (meaning *not to eat)* in the second:

_____

_____

22. But *fast* can also have another meaning. It can also transform itself into a thing. When it takes on this meaning, it is equivalent to a *prolonged period when someone does not eat.* So write a third sentence here using it in that way:

_____

_____

23. Now let's play with the Picture Word *fly*. In its first sentence, let it be an action:

_____

_____

24. Now let's change its picture. Let's make it into a thing – in this case, a *small insect:*

_____

_____

25. Now let's change its picture again. Let's give it a different meaning. This time let's make it into a detail Picture Word – detail of a thing, but putting it into this sentence:

"Johnny hit a _____ ball, but it was caught by the center fielder."

26. So we can agree by now that Picture Words can change their meanings over and over again. There are probably thousands of them that can go from one meaning to another, depending on how they are used in each individual sentence. Think of five more that have more than one meaning, and write them here:

_____

_____

27.   We will, of course, come back to Picture Words, and their shifting meanings, over and over again in this book. But right now, we should take a closer look at our second kind of word – the *Connecting Word.*

A Picture Word is a Picture Word because it has a built-in picture in it. But a Connecting Word has no built-in _____ in it.

28.   Therefore, when you say a Connecting Word by itself, you don't see anything at all. This is because unless you put it in a sentence, unless you join it up with a Picture Word, it gives you no _____ at all.

29.   What does it do, then? The answer is contained in its name. A Connecting Word shows how the Picture Words _____ to each other.

30.   A Connecting Word is a word that shows us the _____ between our Picture Words.

31.   In the next chapter, we'll go over the different kinds of Connecting Words that we have available. And we'll practice putting them in between our Picture Words to show exactly how these Picture Words relate to each other.

Right now, however, we need only a brief summary of what you've learned in this chapter. You've learned, first of all, that there are only _____ main kinds of words.

32.   The first main kind of word has a built-in picture, and is therefore called a _____ Word.

33.   The second main kind of word shows the relations, or connections, between these Picture Words, and is therefore called a _____ Word.

34.   That's all the kinds of words we need to build all the sentences in the world. Two kinds of words: _____ Words, and _____ Words.

Now go on to Chapter 2, and we'll see our first step in putting them together to tell other people our thoughts.

Chapter 2

How to Put These Two Word–Parts Together to Write a Single Sentence

N OW, ONCE AGAIN, what we do with these word-parts – these Picture Words and Connecting Words – is this: We put them together.

We put them together to tell other people our thoughts.

We put them together into *those larger units of thought* that we call *sentences.*

We have three steps: First, we have the word-parts themselves. Then we string those word-parts together to form larger units of thought called sentences. And then we string these sentences together to form even larger units of thought called communications – stories, or explanations, or business reports, or poems.

Thus, by building words into sentences, and sentences into stories, we share our thoughts with other people.

In the last chapter, we examined the first step – the word-parts themselves. In this chapter and the next, we're going to examine the second step – building these word-parts into a single sentence. And then, starting in Chapter 4, we're going to examine the final step – stringing those sentences together so that they make sense. So that other people understand them. Share them. Act on them.

This is all there is to grammar, or writing, or communication. This is how we tell other people our thoughts.

So we are now on the second step. We are now about to take our two kinds of words, and use them to build our next larger unit of thought, the sentence.

Now, what is this *sentence?* It is simply *as much of your thought as you can effectively give the other person at one time. So that he can understand this part of your thought the moment he hears it. And then pass on to the next.*

Once again, you are trying to tell someone else your thoughts. But you can't tell him all of your thoughts at one time. There are simply too many of them. So you tell them to him thought by thought.

And each of these individual thoughts is a sentence.

You choose these sentences, one by one. You compose them, one by one. You make them up, out of the Picture Words and the Connecting Words that you have on hand.

You choose your Pictures. And you choose your Connections. And you put them together, *to make as much of a thought as you believe the other person can understand at one time.*

And then you pause. You pause for a second, to let her absorb this one thought before you go on to the next.

If you are writing, you put in a period at the end of that sentence, to mark that pause.

If you are speaking, you let your voice lapse for a second, to mark that same pause at the end of each sentence.

This gives her mind a chance to go over that sentence – to go over that thought – and understand it. And then you go on to the next sentence. To the next thought.

Always, of course, your goal is to be understood. You want to transmit pictures – thoughts – ideas – beliefs – from your mind to her mind. And you want to transmit them as precisely as possible.

Let's see how you do this.

You have your Picture Words, and you have your Connecting Words. Now you begin sorting them out.

First you turn to the Picture Words. You ask yourself: *"What are the pictures I want to convey in this sentence? How detailed should these pictures be? Which of them should be put in this sentence, and which should be left over for the next sentence?"*

I can show you best how this process works by taking the simplest example. Let's say that you want to tell someone a story. You want to tell him what happened to you the day before. And you want him to see what you saw, feel what you felt, experience what you experienced.

You would probably start, then, by locating the story for him in time. To do this, you would choose the Picture Word *Yesterday.* And he would know exactly what day you were talking about – exactly on what day your story began.

Next, you would want to tell him who the story was about. So you would choose the Picture Word *I.* And he would again follow your train of thought perfectly.

Next, you would want to tell him what it was that you did. So you would choose the Picture Word *hit.* And he would still understand the word-picture you are giving him, as you develop it part by part.

Then, finally, you would want to tell him who it was that you hit. So you would choose the Picture Word *Harry.* And this would finish your first sentence – your first thought. And he would have understood it completely.

Thus, you have chosen four Picture Words: *"Yesterday, I hit Harry."* You have used them to transmit a simple, direct, visual thought. You have gained your listener's attention. You have set a stage for your story. You can now go on with your next sentence, to continue that story.

But let's not go on yet. Instead, let's look at that first sentence again, more carefully.

In the first place, you have built this sentence using nothing but Picture Words. You were able to do this because your thought was so direct, and so simple, that you needed no extra Connecting Words to make it perfectly clear.

However, it is only rarely that you can write any sentence without Connectors. As we shall see in a moment, if you want to express more complicated thoughts, you will have to use them.

(In fact, one of the great differences between early man

and the civilized person is that early man did not use Connectors, and the civilized person does. Early man said, for example, "Me want drink water." The civilized person adds two Connectives, and says, "I want *a* drink *of* water." This speech is not only more "proper." It is clearer. We understand it more easily, and more immediately.)

Secondly, the thought you have transmitted using these Picture Words, *"Yesterday, I hit Harry"* – is still rather bare. It is almost an outline-thought. You can use many more Picture Words, if you so choose, to put more details into it.

You can, for example, take any of the four words in this sentence, and make them much more detailed and more vivid. Like this:

You can make *Yesterday* more detailed by saying *Yesterday morning*. Or (if you want to add a Connecting Word) you can say, *Yesterday morning at eleven o'clock*.

You can take *I* and elaborate on it in several ways. You can express cause-and-effect by saying *Yesterday, because I was at my wit's end, I* ... (Notice again that you are not only adding more Picture Words, but also Connecting Words.)

Or, you can add inner emotion by saying *Yesterday I finally* ...

Or you can emphasize your determination by starting out this way: *Yesterday, I decided that no matter what the consequences, I was going to* ...

So you have taken one of the Picture Words in your sentence, *I*, and elaborated on it in three different ways. To do this, you have added more Picture Words and Connecting Words, to get as much detail into the sentence as you need.

You can do the same with the other two words. You can, for example, change *hit* to a stronger Picture Word, say, *smashed*, or *socked*. Or you can add more Picture Words and Connecting Words to it – such as: *Yesterday, I hauled off and hit* ...

And you can do the same thing to poor old Harry. You can say, for example, *that low-down, miserable, son-of-a-gun, Harry*. And – through all these variations and elaborations – your listener will still understand you perfectly.

The decision is up to you. By expanding or contracting

your pictures, you control the amount of detail that your listener gets from each sentence.

But there is, of course, a goal that you want to achieve from this sentence – and from every other sentence you write. And that goal is, once again, to be immediately understood.

This goal tells you how much detail you can put into that sentence. And it also tells you how to arrange the detail that you do put into it.

For example, if you put all the details we've looked at into that sentence, it would get quite unwieldy. Like this:

"Yesterday morning at eleven o'clock, I, because I was at my wit's end, decided that, no matter what the consequences, I was going to haul off and hit that low-down, miserable son-of-a-gun, Harry."

We have all seen sentences like this one. And we have all been confused by them. But we have never known why before, or how to correct them.

So let me show you the right way to put your Picture Words together, in whatever detail you want, without confusing your reader.

What you need to know, of course, is how to use your second main word-part, the *Connectors.*

These Connecting Words, as we've already seen, are entirely different from the Picture Words we've been using. Those Picture Words all had a built-in image within them. You could say them alone *(hit ... yesterday ... Harry),* and you would automatically see a picture.

However, when you say a Connecting Word alone, you see no picture at all *(a ... and ... in ... when ... if).* They are almost invisible words, whose main purpose is to connect your Picture Words in the right order.

So, when you start to compose your sentence, you first choose your pictures. And then you choose the Connecting Words that link up these pictures in the most easily understood order.

Let's look at some of these Connecting Words now. And see what kinds of connections, links, "road maps" they allow you to build into your sentence for your listener.

Some Connecting Words tell your listener where your pictures go in *space*. For example, if you wanted to tell *where* you hit Harry, you would choose the Connecting Words *in* and *the,* and then the additional Picture Word *face.*

This would allow you to say, *"Yesterday I hit Harry in the face."* And your listener would know exactly where your blow had landed.

There are, fortunately, many Connecting Words for space. Some of them are: *on … over … under … to … from … above … below …* etc.

Then there are the Connecting Words that tell your listener where your pictures go in *time.* For example, you could add more detail to your sentence about Harry by choosing the Connecting Words and *then.* Put in a few more pictures, and you get this: *Yesterday I hit Harry, and then I hit him again."*

There are also many other Connecting Words for time. Some of them are: *before … after … until … during … when …* etc.

Then there are the Connecting Words that tell your listener how your pictures relate to each other as *cause-and-effect.* For example, to give the cause of your hitting poor old Harry, you might choose the Connecting Word *because,* and go on from there like this: *"Because I could stand it no longer, I hit Harry yesterday."*

Some other Connecting Words that show cause-and-effect are: *since … if … as* (example: *As a result, I hit him) … for* (example: *I hit him for this reason) …* and so on.

Then there are Connecting Words that tell your listener that the pictures in your sentence are *identical.* That one is a substitute for the other. For example, if you wanted to tell your listener more about why you hit Harry, you might choose the Connecting Word *is.* And then restructure your sentence like this: *"Harry is a snake, so I hit him yesterday."*

Other Connecting Words that show identity are: *am … are … was … were … has been … will be …* and so on. In fact, about a third of all sentences we use are built around just such identity Connectors. As we shall see, this is especially true when we instruct someone else, or explain how to do something.

Then there are the Connecting Words that *point out* certain Picture Words. That tell your listener that this is the particular boy, or woman, or ship that you're talking about in this sentence. For example, you could choose the Connecting Word *the* to distinguish Harry from all other snakes in the world. And come up with this sentence: *"Harry is the snake I hit yesterday."*

Other Connecting Words that point out specific Picture Words are: *that ... this ... these ... those ...* and so on.

Incidentally, these *pointer-Connectors* are especially powerful in removing confusion. For example, sometimes the same Picture Word can mean either a thing or an action (such as the word *sail* which we used in a previous example). Therefore, you have to tell your listener whether you're using it as an action, or as a thing, in the particular sentence you are now communicating to him. You do this simply by inserting a pointer-Connector in front of it *(the sail)*. Immediately, your listener knows it is a thing. And you have eliminated any possible confusion.

Then there are the road-sign Connectors. These Connecting Words tell your listener the *direction* in which your thought flow is about to go.

Some of these *road-sign* Connectors (like *and* and *then)* say, *"Go straight ahead – no contradiction coming."* For example: "Yesterday I hit Harry, *and then* I hit him again."

Other road-sign Connectors (like *but* and *however)* give your listener an entirely different message. They say, *"Warning! Contradiction coming. Thought-flow about to change direction."*

For example: "Yesterday I hit Harry, *but* today we're friends."

Equally important, these road-sign Connectors not only tell your listener the direction in which your pictures, and thoughts, flow within your sentence; they also tell her the direction your thoughts flow from one sentence to the next.

So you use them, not only to connect pictures together, but also to connect sentences together. They do double duty. And you will learn to value them as one of the most powerful instruments you have to make sure other people understand your thoughts.

Some other examples are: *also ... although ... still ... instead ...* and so on.

These, then, are some of the main kinds of Connecting Words available to you. There are a few others. But they are mainly used between sentences, rather than inside them. So we will meet them later, when we want to put them to work.

As you can see, most of these Connecting Words are quite small, and almost invisible. We usually notice them only when they are linked up with a Picture Word, and therefore form part of its overall image.

Yet they perform a vital role for us, because they let us arrange our Picture Words in the precise order we need, to allow other people to understand them.

This, once again, is the goal of communication: to have other people understand our thoughts. Now we have examined both the tools we have to do this – our Picture Words and our Connecting Words.

And we have seen how to put these two kinds of words together, to produce that larger unit of thought we call the sentence.

Now let's go one step further, and learn a few working rules that make every one of these sentences as easily understood as possible.

**Exercises and Applications
for Chapter 2**

THIS GROUP of exercises is the longest and the most important in the book. The reason for this is simple: It gives you over 50 of the almost-invisible Connecting Words, and shows you how they can add clarity and punch to everything you say.

The trouble with these Connecting Words, of course, is that they don't have built-in pictures within them. Therefore, they are almost invisible. In our everyday use of language, we usually don't even see them.

What we do see, usually, is our Picture Words. They contain the things, actions, colors, smells, sounds, feelings, judgments, ideas, and details. And, at first glance, that seems to be all there is to language.

But these Picture Words have to be put together. They have to be related to each other. They have to be arranged in space and time, and then in sequence and importance, and identity.

And these relations add as much meaning to your sentences as the Picture Words themselves.

1. This can be illustrated quite simply. Let's take two sentences, both of which have the same Picture Words, but different Connecting Words. And let's see how the meaning of the entire sentence changes as we change these Connecting Words:

"I went *into* the house."

"I went *out of* the house."

Here is the same person, the same action, the same object. But the relation between the three – and therefore the meaning of the sentence – has been completely changed by simply switching Connectors.

So we know that these relationships are vital to our sentences. And we know that each new Connecting Word gives us a new relationship.

So, as we explore the Connecting Words in these exercises, we pick up dozens of marvelous tools to express our thoughts more clearly and more precisely than we could without them.

Let's start with Connecting Words that express relationships in *space*. They arrange two or more Picture Words for us so that we can see them, or feel them, in physical space.

The first of these is the one we have already used, *in*. *In* tells us that one Picture Word (and the thing it represents) is *contained* within another.

Let's make these Connecting Words stand out. To do this, let's put them at the very beginning of each sentence. So write a sentence here starting with *in:*

---

2.   A classic example of such a sentence is one from the Bible: "In my Father's house are many mansions."

Try to keep your sentences as short and simple as this. All you are trying to do is see the Connecting Word, and examine the relationship it contains, so that you may become more aware of what it can do for you in constructing your own sentences.

Now, there are other Connecting Words that come out of *in*. Two of them, in fact. The first is *into*. *Into* tells you that one Picture Word is *going* into another. So write a sentence here starting with *into:*

The classic example here is probably: "Into the Valley of Death rode the six hundred." It shows that such shifts from the ordinary sentence structure are not only enlightening, but also effective.

3.   The third Connecting Word in this *in* group is *inside*. Notice that it combines a Connecting Word *(in)* with a

Picture Word *(side)* to give us a new Connector. *Inside* is another way of telling us that one Picture Word is contained within another. So write a sentence here starting with *inside:*

_____

_____

4.   Now I think you have the idea. So let's go through the rest of the space Connectors in alphabetical order. Do as many or as few of them as you wish. I've simply listed as many of them as I could find for you here, so you can have them available when you want to use them.
      The first is *above.* Write *your* above sentence here:

_____

_____

5.   *Against.* Write your *against* sentence here:

_____

_____

6.   *Among.* Write your *among* sentence here:

_____

_____

7.   *At.* Write your *at* sentence here:

_____

_____

8.   *After* presents us with not only one Connecting opportunity, but two. It can be used to connect Picture Words in space, such as: "The bakery shop is located between here and the corner, right *after* the shoemaker's."
      Here, of course, it means *situated directly behind* something else. But *after* can also be used to connect Picture Words in time. For example: *"After* it rained, the sky cleared." Here it means *following directly behind* some other event.

So we can use *after* both ways. It gives us two valuable links with which to build our thought-chains. Let's use it the first way right now. Write your *after* sentence here:

_____

_____

9.   *Before* also can be used to connect Picture Words in either space or time. Use it here as a space Connector:

_____

_____

10.   *Behind,* however, can only be used as a space Connector. So used, it is often interchangeable with *after.* Write your *behind* sentence here:

_____

_____

11.   *Between* tells us that one Picture Word is *located in the space interval (or time interval) bounded by two others.* Use it here as a space Connector:

_____

_____

12.   *By* comes next. Write your *by* sentence here:

_____

_____

13.   Now write a sentence starting with *down:*

_____

_____

14.   Now write a sentence starting with *from:*

_____

_____

15.   Now write a sentence starting with *near*:

_____

_____

16.   Now write a sentence starting with *of*:

_____

_____

17.   Now write a sentence starting with *off*:

_____

_____

18.   Now write a sentence starting with *on*:

_____

_____

19.   Now write a sentence starting with *over*:

_____

_____

20.   Now write a sentence starting with *to*:

_____

_____

21.   Now write a sentence starting with *toward*:

_____

_____

22.   Now write a sentence starting with *under*:

_____

_____

23.   Now write a sentence starting with *up*:

_____

_____

24. Now write a sentence starting with *with*:

_____

_____

25. Now write a sentence starting with *within*:

_____

_____

26. Now write a sentence starting with *without*:

_____

_____

27. Wonderful! You now have at least twenty-six single word space Connectors to use in building your sentences. Twenty-six different ways in which to arrange your Picture Words in space.

But these are only the beginning. In addition to these one-word space Connectors, our language has also given us multi-word space Connectors. Here, for example, are some of them:

Along with ... Apart from ... As far as ... Back of ... In addition to ... In view of ... Together with ... And so on.

Now, it might be fun to play with these space Connectors for a moment before we leave them. One of the best games is simply to take the same Picture Words, and run them through a whole stream of Connectors, one after the other. Like this:

Let's take the Picture Words *boat* and *river*. Let's modify both of them with the point-out Connector *the*. So we have *the boat* and *the river*. And then let's add *is*, and end up with: "The boat is _____ the river."

Now we can start arranging and rearranging these two images in all sorts of ways. I'll give you the Connectors. You fit the sentences.

28. *In:* _____

29. *Below:* _____

30. *Near:* _____

31. *Out of:* _____

32. *Away from:* _____

33. *In view of:* _____

34. And so on. All these sentences make sense. Though some of them are a little ridiculous at first glance.

But did you see the way that poor boat bounced around in space, as we changed one Connector for another? This game is not only fun, but – especially for children – valuable. Because it gives them marvelous practice in rearranging images to fit (or create) new kinds of reality.

And, incidentally, did you notice three new space Connectors in this game *(below, out of, away from)* that were not included in the first list? New ones emerge all the time as you become aware of their presence. The sharper your eyes grow, the more astounded you become at the almost limitless wealth of your own language.

So we've now explored the space Connectors. You'll discover more of them, of course. So here's some space to write them in as you do:

_____

_____

35. Now we turn to our second kind of Connecting Word the Connector that relates our Picture Words in *time.* There are fewer of these, but they are equally important.

The first we will discuss here is *after.* Before we used it as a space Connector. Here it is used as a time Connector. Start a sentence with it here:

_____

_____

36. Now start a sentence with *before:*

_____

_____

37. Start a sentence with *during:*

_____

_____

38. Start a sentence with *when:*

_____

_____

39. Start a sentence with *until:*

_____

_____

40. Start a sentence with *as:*

_____

_____

41. Start a sentence with *while:*

_____

_____

42. Start a sentence with *since:*

_____

_____

43. Start a sentence with *as long as:*

_____

_____

44. Now, let's play the same kind of game with these time Connectors that we did with our space Connectors. This time let's take the sentence: "_____ he drank, she cried." And then run the nine time Connectors listed above through this sentence.

The first one would be: *"After he drank, she cried."*

Do the rest here:

45. *Before* _____

46. *During* _____

47. *When* _____

48. *Until* _____

49. *As* _____

50. *While* _____

51. *Since* _____

52. *As long as* _____

53. Eight of these nine sentences make sense. One does not. It is, of course, "During he drank, she cried." It doesn't sound right to you, and it isn't.

But you can easily change it to sound right. Do that here:

_____

_____

54. Now they all sound right. Your ear automatically brought the odd one into line, just as it does when you write or speak your everyday thoughts.

Now go over the nine sentences again, and see how the different Connectors change them. Notice that not only time, but meaning changes from sentence to sentence.

There is a vast difference, for example, between *"After he drank, she cried"* and *"Before he drank, she cried."* The Picture Word, *drank,* remains the same in both sentences. But in the first sentence, you get the impression that it is bad for him. And in the second sentence, that it is good for him.

So, once again, meaning in any sentence is always a combination of Picture Words and Connecting Words.

Relationship (carried by the Connecting Words) adds as much to meaning as image (carried by the Picture Words).

This is vital. Which is why we keep coming back to it again and again.

Again, you don't usually see the Connecting Words. And

much of learning how to communicate (which is the goal of all grammar) consists in recognizing them, and using them to their best advantage.

55.   One other fact about these time Connectors may interest you. There are far fewer of them than there are of the space Connectors.

For example, we've listed over forty space Connectors in this exercise so far. But only nine time Connectors. (Plus two more we'll discuss in a minute.)

Why? Probably because space is different from time. And language unconsciously reflects that difference.

Space surrounds us in all directions. It is up and down, on both sides, and at all angles.

Time, however, proceeds in a straight line. On that line (as far as we know now) are only three possible positions: before, during, and after.

So there are dozens of words we can use to express the various relations and arrangements that can occur in space. But far fewer that will express those three positions in time.

56.   And now, talking about movement, we come to the two most important time Connectors of all. They are, of course, *and* and *then*.

These are the Connectors we use when we talk about movement forward in time. Something happens, *and then* something else happens after it. We show our reader that these two events are connected in time, one after the other by *and* ... or *then* ... or both, *and then*.

(*And* is also used as a space Connector, of course. When it is so used, it means one thing is added to another. Just as when it is used as a time Connector, it means that one event is added to another.)

They are probably two of the most useful, and therefore most widely used words in our language. So let's put them to work right now.

First write a sentence using *and* as a space Connector. This sentence does not have to start with *and:*

_____

_____

57.   Now write a sentence using *and* as a time Connector. Make it connect two events, rather than two objects:

_____

_____

58.   Now write a sentence using *then* as a time Connector.

_____

_____

59.   Now write two sentences, and use *then* to connect them. Use *then* as the first word of the second sentence:

_____

_____

60.   You see at once, of course, that *then* makes a marvelous way to tie one sentence into the one before it. It is a perfect link between sentences, as well as within them. We will come back to this fact quite often.
   Now write a sentence using *and then* as a time Connector.

_____

_____

61.   Now write two sentences using *and then* as a time Connector. Start the second sentence with *And then:*

_____

_____

62.   So, when we move our thoughts forward through time, we use as our most common Connectors *and* and *then.* They show that something happened, *and then* that something else happened after it.
63.   But there are other ways of connecting events besides their simple order in time. They may also be connected, for example, by *cause-and-effect.*
   And there is a whole group of Connecting Words that

express these cause-and-effect relationships. Let's examine them now:

The first is *because*. We've already used it to express a cause-and-effect relationship in this sentence: *"Because* I could stand it no longer, I hit Harry yesterday."

Now you write a *because* sentence here:

_____

_____

64. The next cause-and-effect Connector is *since*. There are two meanings to the word *since*. The first is as in *"Since 1983 I've wanted to hit Harry."* The second is as in *"Since Harry is such a lowlife, I finally couldn't resist."* The first is a time Connector. The second is a cause-and-effect Connector. Write an example of the second here:

_____

_____

65. The next cause-and-effect Connector is *as*. It is often simply substituted for *because* or *since*. Write your *as* sentence here:

_____

_____

66. But *as* is more correctly used in a cause-and-effect phrase. Such a phrase is *as a result of.* Write a sentence using that phrase here:

_____

_____

67. The next cause-and-effect Connector is *for.* Usually, when we use *for,* we actually mean *for this reason.* Thus, when we say, "I went out *for* a book," we really mean, "I went out for this *reason:* To get a book."

Write your *for* sentence here. It can either start with *for,* or have it in the middle:

_____

_____

68.   The next cause-and-effect Connector is *thus*. When *thus* is used within a sentence, it is usually accompanied by *and*. When it is used between two sentences, the *and* is usually dropped.
Write a single sentence using *and thus:*

_____

_____

69.   Write two sentences connected by *thus*. Start the second sentence with *thus:*

_____

_____

70.   *Therefore* is often used instead of *thus*. Write a single sentence using *therefore*. (You will find you want to add *and* to it again.)

_____

_____

71.   Now write two sentences linked by *therefore:*

_____

_____

72.   The next cause-and-effect Connector is *if*. *If* is a very special cause-and-effect Connector, for this reason:
All the other cause-and-effect Connectors link events that have already happened. For example: *"Because he hit me, I fell down"* – both past. Or: *"Since I'm broke, I'll have to get a job"* – both present.
All these events have happened, and are therefore certain. But *if* deals with the future, with events that have not yet happened, and that are therefore uncertain.
If, therefore, allows us to explore possible futures. *If* shows us that the world is not permanently fixed in any one mold. But that it may be shaped - at least partially- by ourselves as we encounter it.

So *if* is a precious tool. And should be so cherished, and used as often as possible to probe the future.

Write your *if* sentence here. Start this sentence with *if:*

_____

_____

73.   Now write a sentence with *if* in the middle:

_____

_____

74.   Another kind of uncertain cause-and-effect Connector is *unless*. Write your *unless* sentence here.

_____

_____

75.   So we have cause-and-effect that is certain *(because ... since ... therefore)*. And cause-and-effect that is uncertain *(if)*. One allows us to explore the present, and seek out its chain of causes in the past. The other allows us to test the future, and anticipate the effects our plans for it will bring us.

76.   So we now have two ways of relating the events that occur within our sentences (and between them): Time sequence, and cause-and-effect.

But they are only a fraction of the total number of relations that exist, ready-made for us, in our language. And that we can use to tie together our pictures to express the complicated and ever-changing universe that surrounds us.

Let us examine some of these other Connectors now. And test briefly the possibilities they open up for us.

One of the most important of them is the group of *road-sign Connectors*. These are the Connecting Words that show your reader the *direction that your flow of thought is going to take* within your sentence, and from one sentence to the next.

We have already met two of them: *and* and *then*. These

are, of course, primarily time Connectors. They show that the events in your sentence (or sentences) are following each other, one after the other, down the straight and narrow path of time.

But they also show your reader something more. *They also show your reader that your thought-flow is also continuing on in a straight line.* That what you are going to say next (after you use *and,* or *then*) is going to add on to what you've said before. And, most important of all, that they will not contradict each other.

They are, therefore, a road sign for your reader. A road sign that says, *"Straight thought-flow ahead. No changes in direction."*

But now let's contrast them with another road-sign Connector: *but.* What does *but* say to your reader? This: *"Warning! Change in direction! U-turn ahead!"*

We can show this by a simple example. Let's take a sentence that revolves around the straight-line, go-ahead relationship between two thoughts, expressed by *and.* Like this: "He is a nice man, *and* I am going to marry him."

There is no surprise here. The second part of the sentence carries out the first exactly. It delivers exactly what the *and* promises the reader. Everyone is happy.

But now let's write another, similar sentence. This time, however, revolving around the U-turn relationship expressed by *but.* Like this: "He is a nice man, *but* I can't marry him."

Here are two thoughts that contradict each other. Yet you want to put them in the same sentence, in order to lead your reader into your story. It is evidently a complicated story. And to keep her from getting lost in the middle of it, you give her a road sign: *but.*

But shows her that there are twists and turns in the story. That it is not just a simple straight line. And, therefore she is prepared for the turns before she hits them.

So, again, these Connecting Words reflect reality, and give us ways to deal with it. Life is not simple, but complicated. It is not lived, or experienced, in a straight line, but through a series of twists and turns.

And we need words to reflect these turns. And we have them in our road-sign Connectors.

77.   Now let's put these road-sign Connectors to work. The most common road-sign Connectors, of course, are *and* and *then*. So write a sentence here, using *and then* in its middle, to show your reader that one thought is following in a straight line from another (like this: "I went for a walk, *and then* took a cab back home."):

_____

_____

78.   Now use *and then* as a road-sign Connector to link two sentences together in a straight-line flow of thought. Start the second sentence with *and then:*

_____

_____

79.   Now use *then* alone in the middle of a sentence, to link two thoughts in a straight line within that sentence:

_____

_____

80.   Use *then* to link two sentences together. Start the second sentence with *then:*

_____

_____

81.   There are other words that can be used with *and* to link your thoughts together. One of them is *now* – which gives us *and now.*

And now also tells your listener that your thought is proceeding ahead in a straight line. Use it here to link two sentences together:

_____

_____

82. Then we have *and so*. This road-sign Connector is doubly valuable, since it combines straight-line thought-flow *(and)* with cause-and-effect *(so)*.

This time, use *and so* in the middle of a sentence, to connect two thoughts within it:

---

83. So we have these straight-line Connectors so far: *and ... and then ... and now ... and so.* I think you understand now how they work.

But they only scratch the surface of the number of straight-line Connectors that our language provides for us. Let me list several others here, so you can use them whenever you need them:

Again ... also ... and also ... as well ... besides ... beyond that ... equally important ... further ... furthermore ... in addition ... likewise ... moreover ... next ... now ... on top of that ... above that ... over and above that ... so ... or ... and so on.

As you can see, some of these straight-line Connectors have one word, and some have more. Some are made of pure Connecting Words. Some have Picture Words in them as well.

But they all have the same purpose: To show your reader, in advance, that the thought that's coming is going in the same direction as the thought that just passed.

84. Thus, they do a different job from our next kind of road sign Connector. This is the road-sign Connector (like *but*) that signals your reader in advance that a change of direction is coming.

That change may be a complete U-turn, such as *but*. Or, it may be a lesser change in direction, such as *still*. In any case, the reader is forewarned, and a possible confusion prevented.

So use *but* here to turn your flow of thought around in midsentence:

_____

_____

85.   Now use *but* to link two sentences. Start the second sentence with *but:*

_____

_____

86.   Now use *still* to link two sentences:

_____

_____

87.   Now use *however* to link the two:

_____

_____

88.   Now use *although:*

_____

_____

89.   And now use *though:*

_____

_____

90.   So now you get the idea. There are, however, dozens of ways to shift the direction of your thought-flow, both within and between sentences. Let me list a few more of them for you here:

And yet ... even so ... for all that ... in contrast ... nevertheless ... on the contrary ... on the other hand ... otherwise ... yet ... and so on.

So we have road-sign Connectors that say *"Go ahead."* And we have road-sign Connectors that say *"Change direction."*

These are the two main kinds of road-sign Connectors. But there are others. Road-sign Connectors that say *"Let's sum up.* " Or road-sign Connectors that say *"Let's look at this (or these)."*

But these Connectors are used mainly between sentences. So we won't go into them here.

Instead, we'll look now at our next main kind of Connecting Word. In order to do so correctly, let's review for a moment:

We've seen that these Connecting Words may be used in two main ways: To link our Picture Words. And to link up the more complete thought fragments that we make up from these Picture Words.

Communication, therefore, is somewhat like correctly fitting together a puzzle. We take the pieces that are given to us, our Picture Words and our Connecting Words, and we fit them together accurately in space. And then we fit them together accurately in time.

And if there is a cause-and-effect relationship between them, we also put that in.

So we are linking together a chain of words, to share with another person our view of reality.

She follows along behind us on the chain, absorbing our thoughts as we give them to her in our words. Since we don't want her to get lost, or step off the chain, we also put in road signs along the way for her. So she knows where we are going, before we actually go there.

And so she knows exactly where our pictures, and images, and thoughts are, in space, and time, and cause and-effect.

But there is another relationship we must also give her, if she is to understand us completely. And that is the *identity* or *meaning* of our most important Picture Words.

91.   There are at least three occasions when you have to give Picture Words a new meaning for your reader. They are:

1. When you are describing a unique object. Like a girl you love. And you have to tell him what her eyes are like.

And what her hair is like. And what her voice is like.

2. When you introduce a new word. Or a new idea. Or a new definition. And you have to tell him what that new word is, in terms of the old words he already understands.

3. Or when you use an old word in a new way. When you give that old word a new twist, a new meaning.

In each of these cases, you are describing something new to your reader. Something he hasn't known before. And that therefore has to be identified for him with something old, something already familiar.

To do this, to make this identity-link, you use a series of identity Connectors.

The most important of them, of course, is *is*. It is the basic identity Connector.

You use *is* on all three occasions we have mentioned above, when you are presenting to your reader something new.

You use *is,* for example, when you are describing a unique object to your reader. You say "His hair *is* chestnut brown." Or, "Her skin *is* as soft as velvet."

Thus, his hair becomes extraordinary. Her skin becomes extraordinary. And the more features of that person you detail for your reader, the more precisely unique that person becomes.

So the first use of the identity Connector is identifying the unique object, in terms of linking it to all the details that make it unique.

92. Now you do it. Give yourself the same problem most professional writers face every day. Pick out a unique object – some person you know well, for example. And write a few sentences here, using *is,* that convey that uniqueness to your reader.

93.   This is the first use of *is*. It can, however, be replaced in such descriptions by another identity Connector, *like*. For example, in this sentence: "When you please her, her voice purrs *like* a cat's."

The two Connectors are, however, slightly different. *Is* shows complete identity – the two Picture Words connected by it are identical in all parts.

Like, on the other hand, shows only partial identity. The two Picture Words connected by it are identical in one part, but not in all parts. The girl's voice and the cat's voice are identical in sound, but in nothing else.

But this limited identity also works. We gain information from it. We visualize the girl more clearly. We come closer and closer to her own true uniqueness.

94.   Now write your own *like* sentence here. Use it to describe the same person you described before by *is:*

---

95.   And there is another partial-identity Connector. It is *as if*. It shows the same partial identity as *like*. For example: "When you please her, her voice sounds *as if* it were purring."

Write your own *as if* sentence here:

---

96.   So this is the use of *is,* and its alternates, in describing unique object.

Now we go on to the use of is in providing the reader with a new definition.

The usual kind of definition, of course, says that some new is really a variation of something old. In other words it explains the new in terms of the familiar.

For example, let us take the definition: "A boy is a male

child." This definition assumes that the reader knows what *male* and *child* mean. But that he doesn't know what *boy* means.

Therefore, the new word *(boy)* is described through a combination of two old and familiar words *(male* and *child).*

We will go into definitions more deeply in Chapter 10. Right now, the important fact for you is that *is* serves as the Connecting Word in every definition.

97.   Go to the dictionary now, and look up the definitions of two words with which you are not thoroughly familiar. Write them here:

1.

2.

Each of them has to use *is,* of course. You will notice also that the new word is explained in terms of words that should be familiar to you.

If one of the old words in that definition, however, is not familiar to you, then you have to look that up, too. So you keep searching for more and more familiar words. Until all the words in all the definitions you need are familiar to you.

98.   Here's space for one of these double definitions. For a definition that contains a word unfamiliar to you, and therefore requires you to look up that word, too. The next time you encounter one of these, write it here:

1.

2.

----

99.   Now we go to another type of definition. And that is the identification-definition, where both words that are connected by *is* are familiar to your reader. But you are simply saying that one is identical, in this case, with the other. For example: "She *is* my wife."

You are not describing, here. You are defining, or identifying. Both terms of the definition, or identification, are equally familiar. You are simply joining them together, by *is*, to show that they are interchangeable.

Write an identification-definition here. Use it to state a matter of fact:

---

100.   Such identification -definitions can also be used, not only to state matters of fact, but also matters of opinion. For example, "She is a bad girl."

Here the opinion may, or may not, equal the fact. But it is stated as though it were a fact, because of the identity Connector *is*. So *is* is not only a valuable word, but a slippery and perhaps even dangerous one.

Write an opinion sentence here. Feel how it sounds true:

Now, this ability of *is* to express opinion as well as fact is not all bad, of course. It has a marvelous use in our language. And that is to express new meanings for old words, as new facts emerge.

This is the way our understanding of the world grows. Because sometimes our old meanings are wrong, and we get rid of them. And sometimes they are inadequate, and we make them more accurate.

For example, the old meaning of *atom* used to be: *The smallest possible solid piece of a substance.* Today that meaning is: *A miniature solar system that makes up the fundamental building blocks of all substances.*

In the old meaning, the atom was closed and solid. In the new meaning, it is wide open. With the old meaning, it was impossible to change atoms and thus create new substances. With the new meaning, we can do this quite easily.

Thus, a new meaning opens up a whole new world of opportunity to us.

101.   Can you think of other words that have changed their meanings recently? For example: *capitalism, communism,* etc.

Take one of them now, and write both the old and the new definitions here:

Old Definition:

_____

_____

New Definition:

_____

_____

102.   So we have now explored our basic identity Connector, *is.* Now let us look at some of the others.

Is always describes the present. When we want to use an identity Connector to describe the past, however, we use *was.*

Was cannot be used in a definition. Because valid definitions always describe an eternal present. But it can be used in description and identification.

Use *was* here in a descriptive sentence (for example, "His hair *was* steel-gray"):

_____

_____

103.   Now use *was* in a past identification sentence (for example, "She *was* always such a headstrong child"):

_____

_____

104.   Another past identity Connector is *has been*. Use *has been* in a sentence here:

_____

_____

105.   Another past identity Connector is *had been*. Notice the significant difference between it and *has been:*

Has been tells us that something has been identical to something else in the past, and continues to be identical to it right up through the present.

Had been, on the other hand, tells us that something had been identical to something else in the past, but is no longer identical to it at present.

Has been, therefore, is a more permanent fusion of identities. The identity remains, at least through the present.

Had been is, on the other hand, not permanent at all. The identity remained only for a stated time, and then dissolved.

For example, look at the difference between these two sentences:

"She *has been* president of the club for five years now."

"She *had been* president of the club for five years."

The first identity continues. The second has already ended.

Identity Connectors, therefore, like all other Connectors, are like joints that fit Picture Words together. But these fits, the joints, the connections, are not permanent. They can be broken apart, and the Picture Words put together in another way.

So all connections, all relationships, in language are fluid. Just as reality is fluid. And when reality changes, or when we wish to change reality ourselves, we simply take away the old connections and put in new connections.

In this way, our ideas change as the world changes. And we change as the world changes, in order to adapt to it, and use it.

106.   So let's show here that an identification had once

existed, but now exists no longer. Write your *had been* sentence here:

---

107.   But we can also project identifications into the future. We do this by using the identity Connector *will be*.
   Write your *will be* sentence here:

So we now have identity Connectors for past, present and future. We have *is ... was ... has been ... had been ...* and *will be*.

But these Connectors are usually used when we speak about a third person, about someone else rather than you and me. So we now have to go over the identity Connectors we use when we are speaking about you and me.

108.   Let's talk about *you* first. When we talk about what *you* (the person, of course, to whom you are directly speaking) are in the present, we use the identity Connector *are*.

So, right now, write a *you are* sentence here:

---

109.   When we talk about *you* in the past, we use the identity Connector *were*.

So write your *you were* sentence here:

---

110.   Or, when we talk about *you* in the past, we may use the identity-connection *have been*.

Write your *you have been* sentence here:

---

111.   Or, we can also use *had been.*
Write your *you had been* sentence here:

_____

_____

112.   And, when we project *you* into the future, we use the identity Connector *will be.*
Write your *you will* be sentence here:

_____

_____

113.   So those are the identity Connectors for *you.* Now let's examine the ones we use with *I* (the word you use to talk about yourself).
To tell someone else what *I* am in the present, we use the identity Connector, *am.*
Write your *I am* sentence here:

_____

_____

114.   To tell them about *I* in the past, we use the identity Connector *was.*
Write your *I was* sentence here:

_____

_____

115.   Or, we may also use *have been.*
Write your *I have been* sentence here:

_____

_____

116.   Or, we may also use *had been.*
Write your *I had been* sentence here:

_____

_____

117.   And, to project *I* into the future, we may use either of

the identity Connectors *will* or *shall.*

Write your *I will* or *I shall* sentence here:

_____

_____

So we now have identity Connectors for past, present, and future - or I, you, and a third person or thing.

118.   Now we have to have identity Connectors for more-than-one-I *(we)* ... more-than-one-you (which is still *you)* ... and more-than-one-other-person-or-thing *(they, them, these, those,* etc.).

In other words, we want to go from the single to the plural. To do so, in the present, we use the identity Connector *are.* *(We are ... you are ... they are.)*

Write your *we are ... you are ... they are* sentences here:

_____

_____

_____

_____

_____

119.   When we talk about the past, we use the identity Connector *were.*

Write your *we were ... you were ... they were* sentences here:

_____

_____

_____

_____

_____

Or, of course, we can also use *have been,* or *had been.* But you know these well enough now not to need to write them again.

120.   And, to talk about the future, we use our old friend

and identity Connector *will be.*

So write your *we will be* (or *shall be,* if you wish) ... *you will be ... they will be* sentences here:

_____

_____

_____

_____

_____

So there we have our identity Connectors. And they fall right in place with our cause-and-effect Connectors, our time Connectors, our space Connectors, and our road sign Connectors.

121.   We have only one more group of Connectors to go, and we've pretty well explored the entire family.

These are the *pointing Connectors.* They are the Connecting Words that serve as a sort of verbal finger. That point out to your reader that this is the *particular* boy, or woman, or ship, or rock that you are talking about.

The most important of them, of course, is *the. The* serves as a telescope. For example, it picks out of all the women in the world, the one woman you are talking about.

For example: "This is *the* woman I'm going to marry."

Now she can never be confused with any other woman. She is particular, unique.

Like *above* has *below,* or *in* has *out, th*e also has an opposite. It is *a. A* shows us that the Picture Word it connects is not unique. That it is simply one of a whole group of similar objects.

For example, look at the difference in these two sentences:

"This is *a* woman I am taking out."

"This is *the* woman I am taking out."

So *a* serves as a wide-angle lens. With it you see the whole horizon. But *the* telescopes you right in to a particular object on that horizon.

(Or, to put it more technically, *a* tells you that you are considering the whole class of objects designated by any particular Picture Word. *The,* on the other hand, tells you that you are considering only one specific member of that class.)

122.   So let's change a few *a* sentences to *the* sentences, and see what happens.

For example, change these sentences into *the* sentences: "He is a man I know."

_____

_____

123.   "She is a beautiful woman in New York."

_____

_____

124.   "You are a true friend."

_____

_____

125.   In each case, one person becomes paramount. And all the others like him simply fade.

So *the* picks out – selects – makes unique. And it is the quality of selection that also allows us to use *the* to avoid confusion in our sentences. Why? Because some Picture Words, as we have seen, are quite slippery in their meanings. They have more than one meaning, and they often slip from one of these meanings to another without our being aware of it.

The, therefore, is the anchor that holds such words in place in a single meaning. What it does, in essence, is this:

When it connects to a Picture Word, it shows that the word is a thing instead of an action.

Run, for example, means to *move fast.* On the other hand, *the run* means *a long hole in a woman's stocking,* or *a score made at a ballgame.*

Lift means to *raise something. The lift,* on the other hand, is *a British elevator.*

126.   And so on. Why don't you try a few yourself. I'll give you some actions, and you change them into things with *the,* and see how their meanings change at the same moment.

Like this:

Raise: _____

Roll: _____

Help: _____

Sink: _____

127.   And so on. We could go on for hours, of course. The important thing, however, is to notice how these Picture Words relate to each other in meaning, even though they have changed from action to thing.

Sink, for example, means *to go under* something. *The sink* is *a place where water is temporarily stored, and then allowed to go under.*

The meaning carries over, in a slightly altered form, from one embodiment of the word to another. Try it yourself, on the other words above.

So again we see that language, like the universe, is fluid. It changes. One moment it moves, and becomes an action. The next moment it sits still, and becomes a thing.

But the things and the actions are interconnected. We profitably think of them as different states, or manifestations, of the same process.

And language is a tool that helps us see those different processes and changes. And describe them. And understand them. And share them. And even manipulate them.

We do this by naming them with Picture Words, and relating them by Connecting Words. This allows us to take "verbal snapshots" of their shifting meanings. To freeze those meanings for a moment to understand and use them.

And then we go on, if we have to, to break up those old meanings and replace them with ever-new ones.

Reality is fluid. To match it, language is fluid. And much of this fluidity in language, its ability to change, to create new meanings to meet new realities, comes from the Connecting Words we have just described.

These Connecting Words are, in essence, a series of incredibly flexible joints. They allow us to relate our Picture Words to each other in an almost infinite number of ways.

Thus, we can experiment with one new meaning after another – one new expression of our thoughts after another. We do this until we are satisfied that we have the correct one, and that the other person can understand it the moment we tell it to him.

So now we have our first inventory of Connecting Words. These consist of the following:

Space Connectors.

Time Connectors.

Cause-and-Effect Connectors.

Identity Connectors.

Pointer Connectors. And

Road-Sign Connectors.

All of them have a common function. They show how your Picture Words, and even your whole sentences, are *linked* together.

Therefore, let's give them all a common name. Let's call them *Linking Connectors.* Because their primary job is to link together our Picture Words, and then our sentences.

And now let's go on, in Chapter 3, to use these linking Connectors to build a good clear, immediately understandable sentence.

Chapter 3

How to Build Understanding into Every Sentence You Use

ALL RIGHT. You have now learned this first fundamental rule:

To compose a sentence – any sentence – you choose as many Picture Words, and as many Connecting Words, as your listener needs to understand your thought the moment she hears it.

Notice that the goal here is understanding. You want to be understood. You want your listener to be able to absorb that sentence instantly, so she can pass without a moment's trouble onto the next.

In this way, your communication becomes a "series of understandings." And you and your listener are in complete agreement, every step of the way.

And, of course, you want the same understanding to occur within the sentence itself. So you build that understanding into that sentence with every word you put in, or leave out.

This brings up the question: What exactly is *understanding?* And to get the answer to that question, we have to look for a moment at the human mind.

Your mind, and everybody else's mind, may be thought of as a coding and decoding machine. It takes the thoughts within it – let's call them *images* – and codes them into words. And it takes the words it receives from your eyes and ears, decodes them back into images again.

So, every time you build a sentence, realize that the mind of your reader will *not* memorize your words. Instead, it will immediately and automatically translate them into a series of images. And when those images are the same as your images – when those images work the same way for your reader as they do for you – your reader has *understood* you.

You can prove this to yourself quite easily. Let's use the *"Yesterday I hit Harry"* sentence again. A few minutes after you've said it, you then ask your listener, "What did I just say about Harry?"

She replies, "You said that you socked Harry yesterday."

Now, does she understand what you said, despite the fact that she uses the word *socked* instead of your original word, *hit?* Of course. Even though that one word is different, her image is exactly the same as your image.

That's all that counts – understanding, not memorization. No one can memorize everything someone else has told him. We just don't have tape recorder minds. We have image minds. We learn images, and not strings of words.

Why do we memorize images instead of words? For a very good reason: *One image can be memorized as easily as four or six or eight or even ten words.* So instead of storing ten separate facts at once in our memory, we have to store only one.

Think how effective this mental trick is. One simple translation – from words to images – and we cut the amount of memory work needed by as much as 90%.

We *see* what people tell us. Even if it's abstract, we *see* an abstract image. We see what they have seen, and told us about. And then, when we want to tell somebody else about it, we translate those images back out into our own equivalent words.

The same memory trick takes over if you tell someone how to do something. You tell him how to do it in a series of sentences – in strings of words. But, in his mind, he decodes those words and sentences back into images. And then he follows those images to accomplish what you've taught him.

Now, if you want to discover whether he's understood how to perform this task correctly, you're not going to ask him to repeat back to you the words you spoke to him. Because repeating those words means nothing.

What really counts – the only thing that counts – is whether he can do what you want him to do. Whether he can follow the images your words have built in his mind, and perform the string of necessary actions correctly.

If he can – if he does it right – he understood you. If he does it wrong, it doesn't matter how correctly he can repeat your words back to you; those words just aren't giving him the images he needs.

Even in definitions, his words don't have to be exactly the same as yours. You may tell him that the definition of *boy* is *a young man*. And he may then tell you that the definition of *boy* is *a child of the male sex*. His vocabulary uses different words than yours, but you both now share the same image.

Understanding is therefore *image-sharing*. When you and another person understand each other, you share the same images. When the two of you talk about the same things, you both see the same things. When the two of you talk about doing the same actions, you both see how to do those actions.

You have – on that subject, in that area – common minds. You think alike. And that is what communication is all about.

So, when you speak or write, you first turn the images in your own head into words. And when the other person listens to or reads those words, her mind takes them, pauses to translate them into an equivalent image, and then passes on to the next words you are ready to feed her.

This, for example, is the reason you pause after you have said "Yesterday, I hit Harry." This is to allow her to *see* the image that these four words convey. Then, and only then, is she ready for you to go on.

Now, the mind of your reader (or your listener) has certain problems in the translation process we call understanding. And the more you simplify these problems, the more easily you will be understood.

The two basic problems are these:

1.   As we've seen, your reader's mind can retain only

a limited number of words at one time. When it reaches that limit, it must translate those words into an image, and me that image away, before you can go on to give it more words.

2.   To file one of these images away, his mind has to be able to see it fully. A part of that image can't be missing, because then he can see only part of it. And a part image is a hazy image, an unclear image, a forgettable image, and a misunderstood image.

Now let's examine these two problems more closely, and see how we can overcome them.

The first problem, again, is this: Your reader's mind can't handle too many words at one gulp, without converting them into an easier-to-remember image.

We can prove this with the self-destructive expansion of our *"Yesterday, I hit Harry"* sentence. Here it is again:

"Yesterday morning at eleven o'clock, I, because I was at my wit's end, decided that, no matter what the consequences, I was going to haul off and hit that low-down, miserable, son-of-a-gun Harry."

What's the first thing wrong with this sentence? Simply that there are too many words between *I* and *hit* and *Harry*. Let's count them. In this sentence, *I* is introduced in word 6 ... *hit* is word 28 ... and *Harry* is word 33.

Think of it. After you say *I*, your reader has to wade through 21 words before she can discover what *I* am doing in this sentence. Then, after she discovers that *I hit*, she has to go through 4 more words to finally find out that it was *Harry* that *I hit*.

Again, there are 33 words in all until your reader gets a full image of the central action in this sentence. And it is the image of this central action that she has to memorize if she is to understand you.

She just can't do it. Instead of memorizing the central-action image of *I hit Harry*, she's trying to memorize all the intervening details like *at eleven o'clock ... at my wit's end ...* and *no matter what the consequences.*

There's just too much for her memory to absorb at one time. She's trapped at the word level of what you're writing, and she can't compress it into images. She can't see what you're saying, and if she can't see it, she can't understand it.

What is the only thing she can do? Read the sentence through the first time, and admit that she doesn't understand it. And then read it through again, so that – this time – she can hang all the details on the central action.

She has misunderstood you the first time. She tries to correct that misunderstanding the second time. What she probably understands after that second time is the central action, plus one or two of the details. But, because so many words are thrown at her so fast, she will probably forget some of those details.

How can you overcome that first problem? The answer is now obvious. *Cut down the number of words in this sentence.* Take out some of them, and put them in the next sentences that follow. We'll see how in a moment.

The second problem is this: In order to have your reader form a visual image from your words, the *word image* you give him must be complete. And it must be complete within ten words or less.

Why must it be complete within at most ten words? Because his mind can't remember more than ten words before it creates such an image. So, you have to complete that image before that limit.

A sentence, of course, can be made up of several images, but each one of them has to be complete. The rule is simple: At the end of each *word image,* the reader must have enough information to create a *visual image.* And he has to be able to do it within ten words.

So the solution to the second problem fits right into the solution to the first problem. *You make each word image less than ten words, and you make it complete.*

You can see this quite clearly in our *"Yesterday, I hit Harry"* example. Here's how your reader's mind reacts to this sentence:

It first hears *Yesterday,* and converts it into an image. The mind registers the fact that you are not talking about today, or a few hours ago. It rather unconsciously knows that the sun has set, and risen, between this moment and the time you are talking about, twenty-four hours ago.

This is a simple image. It is complete in a single word. It is immediately understood. And filed away.

And your reader's mind is now ready to concentrate on the next part of your sentence.

Now go on to *I hit Harry*. This is a more complicated word-picture. It needs three words to complete it. But when you have finished those three words, your reader's mind has another image to store away.

So, even in this simple sentence of only four words, you have given your reader two images to store away.

But, since you have done it so vividly and concisely, he has had no trouble doing this. You have been immediately understood.

Now the first image in this sentence, *Yesterd*ay, needed only one word to convey its complete picture. But the second image, *I hit Harry,* needed three words. Let's see why:

As I mentioned before, we have all become accustomed to thinking about things in a certain way. We like our thoughts to take a certain form. This form usually follows the pattern of *someone doing something to someone (or something) else.*

In other words, when someone speaks to us, we like first to see an actor ... then an action ... and then the person or thing acted upon, if there is any.

This way of arranging words is not a rule of nature. It is simply an agreement that we have all followed for centuries.

It is a good agreement. It works well. And, since we have all been accustomed to it since we were children, we have now come to expect it from every sentence we hear.

In other words:

We do not consider a sentence to be complete (and therefore understandable) until it fulfills this rule. And if a sentence is made up of more than one image, then at least one of these images must fulfill this rule.

Now, once you know this rule, you know why, once you

have said *I,* you must go on immediately to say *hit.* Because once you have introduced the actor, your listener expects you to follow up immediately with the action.

And you now know why you must follow up *hit* with *Harry.* Because once you have stated an incomplete action, you must immediately complete it. Your listener expects you to do so. She will not understand you – she will not be able to build her image – unless you do.

Now all this is just another way of expressing our basic rule of making each sentence understandable: *Make each word image in that sentence less than ten words, and make, it complete.*

Let's go back to that unreadable expansion of our *Yesterday, I hit Harry* sentence, and see how this could be done. Here is that 33-word sentence again:

"Yesterday morning at eleven o'clock, I, because I was at my wit's end, decided that, no matter what the consequences, I was going to haul off and hit that low-down, miserable, son-of-a-gun, Harry."

Notice how many images there are in this one sentence. This many:

1.   *Yesterday morning at eleven o'clock ...*
2.   *I...*
3.   *because I was at my wit's end ...*
4.   *decided that ...*
5.   *no matter what the consequences,*
6.   *I was going to haul off and hit that low-down miserable, son-of-a-gun, Harry*

I hope you'll agree with me that six separate images in one sentence is too much for any reader to absorb instantly.

And if that weren't bad enough, some of these images block one another. That is, *they intrude into the middle of another image, and prevent it from completing itself in ten words or less.*

So the easiest way of correcting this sentence is just to remove those blocks, and put them somewhere else. Here's one way to do it:

Start with Images 1 and 2: *Yesterday morning at eleven o'clock, I.* Cut out Image 3, and continue with Image 4: *Decided that.* Cut out Image 5, and continue with Image 6: *I was go-*

ing to haul off and hit that low-down, miserable son-of-a-gun, Harry.

So now you have a new two-image sentence that reads:

Yesterday morning at eleven o'clock, I decided that I was going to haul off and hit that low-down, miserable, son-of-a-gun, Harry.

There are still a few too many details in it to be effortlessly clear, but it still is understandable. The risk of *boredom* does enter into it, though, because you may have *given your reader more of those details than she wants.* It would probably have more punch if you pared it down like this:

Yesterday, I hit that miserable son-of-a-gun, Harry.

Either way, the rest of the original sentence (Images 3 and 5) can now be put into a second, three-image sentence, like this:

I decided to do it because I was at my wit's end, and to hit him no matter what the consequences.

What have we seen here? First, that the shorter your images, the easier they are to understand. Too much detail overloads them. It prevents your reader from completing them fast enough to be comfortable with them. This overload-detail, therefore, should be split off into another image or sentence.

Second, if one image blocks the completion of another, both images become impossible to understand. When you find that happening in your first draft, pull out the blocking image, and put it by itself. Give it a separate place in that sentence, or put it in a new sentence of its own.

Always make sure an image or sentence is complete before you go on to the next one. Never allow an image to remain incomplete. Never allow one image to block another. Arrange them as a continuing series of completions, so your reader can understand you every step of the way.

If you send incomplete images, you get back incomplete understandings. If you send complete images, you get back complete understandings. It's as simple as that.

Now only one task remains: To connect each image with the image that precedes it – and then connect each sentence with the sentence that precedes it – so your reader can follow your logic every step of the way.

You do this, of course, with your Connecting Words. The procedure is simple. *Every time you link two images together, they must have a Connecting Word that ties them to each other. And that Connecting Word must be as close to the front of each image as possible.*

Let's see how this rule works by applying it to the two new Harry sentences.

Yesterday, I hit that miserable son-of-a-gun, Harry. I decided to do it because I was at my wit's end, and to hit him no matter what the consequences.

Let's start with the last sentence first. This sentence is made up of three images. They are:

1. *I decided to do it*
2. *because I was at my wit's end,*
3. *and to hit him no matter what the consequences.*

When you wrote this sentence, your job was to connect together these three images as clearly as possible. You did it this way:

You connected the second image to the first by using the Connecting Word *because.*

Then you connected the third image to the second by using the Connecting Word *and.*

This gave you a complete, connected, instantly under-standable sentence. Since the three separate images in it are linked together so strongly, your reader has no trouble following your train of thought perfectly. The "road-sign" Connectors *because* and *and* make sure of that.

And now we go back to the first sentence. This, though even more simple, with only two images, is even more interesting, because here the Connecting Word is invisible.

Yesterday, I hit that miserable son-of-a-gun, Harry.

Now, as you can see, there is no Connecting Word in this sentence. Instead, the necessary connection is provided by the structure of the sentence itself. In that structure, the first image, *Yesterday,* is deliberately open-ended, and therefore needs a second image to give your reader the complete image he demands.

In other words, when you say *Yesterday,* your listener automatically knows that this word-picture is only a prelude. That it is just the introduction to the other word-picture that will immediately follow it.

It is this awareness of his – his automatic expectation that you will immediately add a second word-picture to complete the thought – that provides the connective here.

And, since this open-end sentence pattern is so firmly established in our language, you do not need an actual Connecting Word to convey it to your listener. She picks it up automatically.

(Also, of course, the comma here reinforces the fact that you have something more to say. Or, if you were speaking, you would not lower your voice as completely as you do when you have finished a sentence. And this would give your listener an additional signal that you had not yet expressed your complete thought.)

Now, these "invisible Connectors" occur quite frequently in both our speaking and our writing. They are additional tools to make our meaning clear. We shall therefore touch on many of them in the following chapters.

And, of course, there are many kinds of images in our language that announce immediately that they are open-ended. That they are only an introduction to another part of your complete thought.

In fact, we have several Connecting Words whose main function it is to make just such an announcement to your listener. They are:

When.

For example, *When I left the house, it was raining.*

If

For example, *If you touch me, I'll scream.*

Until.

For example, *Until I met you, I was happy.*

Because.

For example, *Because he was poor, he never had enough to eat.*

And so on.

So, when you use these introductory Connectors, you know that your sentence has to have at least two images in it.

(And if you want it most easily understood, it probably should not have more than two images. Otherwise, you may overload it. But this strategy, also, we will examine in later chapters.)

So those are all the strategies there are for writing a clear sentence. The rest is only application.

You have only three rules to remember. They are:

1. *To compose a sentence, you first combine Picture Words and Connecting Words into complete images.*
2. *You make each image complete in as few words as possible. And you don't let one word-picture interrupt another.*
3. *If your sentence has two or more images in it, you must link them together with a Connector. And that Connector should be as close to the front of the second image as possible.*

These three rules tell you how to write a clear, understandable sentence. With them, you have learned as much as all the years of the old grammar could teach you. And you have learned it more easily, and better.

And now you are about to go beyond anything the old grammar ever dreamed of. You are about to see how to link these sentences together, to give your listener that clear, logical, constantly developing *stream of thought* that we call discourse, or argument, or literature.

NOTE: To introduce you to images, and how to construct and connect them, I have assumed that each image should include an actor and an action, or an identification *(is, was, are, like,* etc.).

This is, however, by no means a necessary rule. It's simply easier to look at images that way first. And it makes the images as large as possible.

I could have, however, made the images smaller by not having each of them include an action or an identification. Any one of them could have had, for example, simply a separate image of two or more words.

In that case, this sentence – *I decided to do it because I was at my wit's end, and to hit him no matter what the consequences* – would have four images instead of three. They would be:

1. *I decided to do it*
2. *because I was at my wit's end,*
3. *and to hit him*
4. *no matter what the consequences.*

Image 4, therefore, would have the Connecting Words *no matter what.*

So there is no hard and fixed rule that tells you how to measure the number of words in an individual image. No more than there is such a rule that tells you how to measure the number of words in an individual sentence.

Language, like the world it reflects, is adaptable. Its images, of course, must be complete, or they can't be instantly understood. But a complete image can be carried best in one case with the actor-action sequence ... and, in another, without it.

The strategy is simple. Write the sentence. Read its images. See if each one of them forms a complete image in your own mind.

If it does, keep it – whether or not it has an actor-action sequence.

The important thing is that it leaps the gap between your mind and your reader's mind. Everything else is simply a tool for doing that.

**Exercises and Applications
for Chapter 3**

For each exercise, either fill in the blank line or circle the correct word or phrase.

Again, let's review. You have taken your two building blocks of communication – Picture Words and Connecting Words – and you have linked them together to form images.

Therefore, from words, you have generated images. And now from these images, you will generate sentences.

And from these sentences, you will then generate entire discourses. Stories, reports, instructions, poems ... a universe of shared emotions and thoughts.

It is all a process of constant building. You start with the simplest words, and end up with the most complicated discourses. But discourses that are organized and therefore immediately understandable from beginning to end.

One step leads logically to another. The same rules apply from start to finish.

Here they are:

1.   This chapter showed you how to put your Picture Words and your Connecting Words together to make images. And then put the images together to make sentences.

The first rule concerns the number of words in each image. Your objective here is to make each image complete with as *(many/few)* words as possible.

2.   If an image has too *(many/few)* words in it, then it will probably confuse your reader.

3.   So don't try to crowd all your details into one image. If you have lots of details to tell your reader, use *(one/two/ more)* images to tell it to her.

4.   You can tell her all the details you want, as you write one image after another, and then one sentence after another. But keep each of those images *(short/long)* and therefore clear.

5.   From time to time, of course, you will write an image,

or a sentence, that is too long. Everyone does it. Then, when you reread it, you will realize it is confusing. And you will want to shorten it.

There are techniques that help you shorten and simplify these overlong word-pictures and sentences. We will discuss them thoroughly in Chapter 6.

Right now, however, the important first rule to remember is this: An image that is too *(long/short)* is also too often misunderstood.

6.   So that's our first rule. Now let's go on to our second. Our second rule deals with this possibility: That one image can sometimes end up in the middle of another one, and therefore block its full meaning.

Thus the first image interrupts the second. It prevents the second image from being *(complete/short)*.

7.   And your reader wants your images to be *(visual/ complete)*. Because only when they are complete can she truly understand them.

8.   So our second rule is this: Don't let one image interrupt another. Always make each image *(interesting/ complete)*.

9.   We have already seen what to do when one image interrupts another. We simply remove the interrupting image, and place it somewhere else.

For example: "And then he saw, as the carriage turned the corner of the road, Melinda running up the road toward him."

Rewrite this sentence here, to remove the block:

_____

_____

10.   There are several ways to do this of course. Here are two:

"And then, as the carriage turned the corner of the road, he saw Melinda running up the road toward him."

"And then the carriage turned the corner of the road. And he saw Melinda running up the road toward him."

Both are correct. Both contain complete images, with no blockage or interruptions. Both are therefore easier to understand than the original sentence I gave you. Which one you choose is a matter of your own personal taste.

The nice thing about language, as about life, is that it has so many ways to be right.

11.   Now, it's important that we ask what causes blockage. Expectation, of course. The fact that we're used to a certain type of sentence structure: Actor ... action ... thing acted upon. And once you start that structure, your reader expects you to complete it as soon as possible.

So, when you introduce an actor, your reader wants *(the action/his name)* right away.

12.   And if the action is not complete by itself, then your reader wants you to *(repeat it/complete it)* as soon as possible.

13.   So now we know why the original sentence above gave the feeling of being blocked, and therefore was hard to understand. Because once we had read the word *he* in it, we wanted to know what it was he was *(claiming/doing)*.

14.   So this too is an easy and evident rule to follow. Once you introduce an actor, then immediately introduce your

_____.

15.   And if the action isn't complete, then _____ it as soon as possible.

16.   And don't let any other images come in between. If they do, put them somewhere else.

17.   So that's our second rule. And now we go on to our third. The third rule talks about the fact that each image has to be connected to the image in front of it. You make this connection – naturally enough – with a Connector.

So our third rule says this: Every two images must be linked together with a *(Picture Word/Connector)*.

18.   And that Connector should come as close to the *(front/back)* of the second image as possible.

19.   Why do you want that Connector as close to the previous _____ as possible? Because, that way,

you tell your reader exactly what type of relationship these two images have to each other. And you tell it to her as soon as possible.

20.   Remember, no image, and no sentence, ever exists by itself. They are always part of an ongoing conversation. They are always connected to other images, and other sentences.

And you always want to show your reader exactly what those connections are. Exactly how these images relate to each other.

And you want to show it to him as *(fast/slowly)* as possible. So he has all the information he needs, in advance.

21.   So get those Connectors up in the _____ of your images. Put them in at the beginning. If you can, start your word-pictures with them.

22.   Once again, we'll have practice doing this in the next chapter, and all the way through Chapter 6.

Right now, however, I just want to point out that there's one kind of Connector that most people automatically put at the beginning of a word-picture or sentence.

And that's the introductory Connectors that we talked about in this chapter. Like *when ... if ... until ... because ...* etc.

23.   For example, when you see *when* at the beginning of a sentence, and that sentence is not a question, then you know that that sentence is going to have more than one image in it.

And you know that its first image is going to be open-ended – that it's going to need another image to complete its thought.

So any sentence that begins with one of these introductory Connectors is sure to have _____ or more images in it.

24.   Now, we've met these introductory Connectors before. We've met some of them as time Connectors. And we've met some of them as cause-and-effect Connectors.

And now we meet them again – but this time as introductory Connectors. Which shows us another marvelous property of our Connecting Words: That they can serve double duty for us, depending on how we choose to use them.

For example, take this sentence:

"I saw Helen when I went downtown."

Here you have a sentence with two images: *I saw Helen,* and *when I went downtown.* They are connected by *when,* which starts the second image.

But there is, of course, another way to write this sentence, so that you start it with *when.* Write that second way here:

_____

_____

25.   This way, you have told your reader about the setting first *(When I went downtown),* and then about the event *(I saw Helen).* Before, you told her about the event first, and then put it in its setting.

Either way is correct. It all depends on the sequence of events that you want your reader to see in your story.

In the first sentence, you use *when* as a straight time Connector. In the second sentence, you use *when* as an introductory Connector.

Either way, it joins two images together. It shows your reader the *(relationship/conflict)* between them.

26.   So Connecting Words can start sentences, as well as the images within them. But, in any case, whenever you have more than _____ images in a sentence, you want to show the relationship between them with a

_____.

27.   So these are our three rules. They show you how to write a good, clear sentence. Like this:

First, you keep all the images you use in that sentence as *(short/long)* as possible.

28.   Second, you don't let one of the images in that sentence *(interrupt/relate to)* another.

29.   And third, if that sentence has two or more images in it, you always tie them together with a *(Picture Word/ Connector)*.

Once you have applied these three rules, you have written a sentence that is clear and understandable. It then serves as a perfect building block of your overall discourse.

And that sentence is now ready to be joined to the sentence before it, and the sentence after it, in a logical and effortless stream of thought.

Chapter 4

How to Link Your Sentences Together

So – YOU NOW know how to link your Picture Words and your Connecting Words together to make images. And you know how to link your images together to make a single sentence. And you also know how to make that sentence clear and understandable, with as much detail in it as it will hold without overloading your listener's mind.

This no-overload factor is, of course, essential. You have found out, in fact, that the art of writing a clear sentence depends as much on what you leave out as on what you put in. There is always a tendency, when you first start to write, to put too much detail into each sentence.

It's as though you wanted to express your complete story in that first sentence. As though you wanted to tell it all, as it were, in one breath.

But, as we've seen, if you put too much detail into a single sentence, your listener can't follow you. His ability to understand you breaks down. You practically hear him shouting at you: "Stop! It's too much at one time! Let me pause for a moment, to understand what you've already said!"

So you do pause. You give him only as much of your thought as you feel is adequate at that time. You call that composed, understandable fragment of your thought a *sentence.* And then you go on, to continue your thought in the next sentence.

Thus – sentence by sentence – understandable thought by understandable thought – you build up your complete Story.

Once again, it's like you were building a "road map" to your thought for your listener. Laying down a line of expected words for her to follow, from your first thought to its end. With little resting stops along the way, called sentences.

Because, when your listener travels along the line of your thought – just as when she travels along a highway – she likes to know where she's going. She asks you to make that journey as easy as possible for her. Which means as predictable as possible.

In other words, when she travels from sentence to sentence of yours, she would appreciate it if there were no surprises, no sudden turns or twists in your flow of thought. She wants every change in direction clearly road-marked for her in advance, nothing that will leave her behind, bewildered and confused.

What she wants from you, then, are bridges. Road signs between one sentence and the next. Verbal road signs that tell her, as soon as possible, that your thought is either continuing in the same direction, or that it's now going to turn.

Fortunately, you have these road signs, all laid out for you in the language itself. They are, primarily, our Connecting Words. The same Connecting Words you've been using up till now. But ready, at this moment, to take on a new task.

You have already used these Connecting Words to link together the Images that made up your sentences. Now you are going to use them to link together the sentences themselves. To link them into a completely understandable flow of thought. So that your listener follows that flow of thought effortlessly, without ever having to figure out by himself where it's going.

You link each two sentences together with this rule (which is simply an extension of the rule you mastered in the last chapter):

Each sentence after the first must have a Connector in it that links it up to the sentence before. And that Connector should be as close to the front of the second sentence as possible.

The first sentence, of course, doesn't need a sentence Connector in it. It starts from zero. It grabs your listener's attention, and opens your story for her.

Therefore, it's completely different from the other sentences in your story. That's why it's often so hard to write. And that's why we put titles, usually, at the front of our stories, or discourses. To tell the listener: "This is what I'm going to talk about now."

Thus, for example, *Yesterday, I hit Harry* is a good first sentence. It sets the scene. Grabs the listener's attention. Is dramatic enough to make him want to hear more.

But, when you have written your first sentence, you must then go on from there. And you must make your second sentence tie into your first.

And you do this by deliberately putting a sentence Connector into that second sentence, to show your listener instantly and precisely how that second sentence relates to the first.

There are three types of sentence Connectors. And you should be able to use them all.

The first type of sentence Connector is the *linking Connector*. It is used here, however, not to connect two word-pictures within a sentence, but two sentences themselves.

Let's see how some of these same linking Connectors can be used as sentence-links, to show your listener just where your thought is going at any moment.

For example:

"Yesterday, I hit Harry. *And then* I hit him again."

Here, the linking Connectors *and then* serve as your sentence-links. They tell your listener that your thought is flowing in a straight line. That you are going to repeat the same action again.

Or as another example:

"Yesterday, I hit Harry. *Because* he's a low-down rat."

Here, the linking Connector *Because* is your sentence-link. It connects, for your listener, the effect to the cause. It tells her why you hit Harry.

Or, as another example:

"Yesterday, I hit Harry. *But* today we're friends."

Here, a "U-turn" road-sign word is absolutely essential. Because your thought has changed direction. Your second sentence contradicts the first. And your listener would run right over the edge of your thought, unless you gave her a road sign to tell her that it was going to make an about-face.

So you used the linking Connector *But.* Because *But* shows her, in advance, that a contradiction is coming. So, when she encounters the words *today we're friends,* she is already expecting them. And you haven't lost her. And she is not confused.

Now, many of the linking Connectors that we've already examined really come into their own when they are used between sentences. In fact, though we have never become aware of this function before, they were really developed by the language in order to serve as sentence-links.

Some of the most important of them are:

Therefore or *thus.* For example: "I am your husband. *Therefore,* I will be faithful to you unto death."

However. For example: "You are a beautiful woman. *However,* you have no soul."

So. For example: "He hit me. *So* I hit him back."

Or. For example: "We can stay in Paris for the night. *Or* we can go on to Versailles."

In fact. For example: "Yes, I like you. *In fact,* I love you."

On the other hand. For example: "Yes, I like you. *On the other hand,* sometimes I don't like you."

At the same time. For example: "Yes, I like you. *At the same time,* I dislike certain of your flaws."

Meanwhile. For example: "So the Third Army broke through in the North. *Meanwhile,* in the South, the enemy lines were also giving way."

For example. For example: "A sentence is a complete thought. *For example,* Yesterday, I hit Harry."

And so on.

Notice that each of the Connectors we have used so far has been placed at the very beginning of the second sentence. This is not at all necessary, of course. Such linking words can just as easily be placed elsewhere in the second sentence. For example:

"Yes, I like you. I *also* like Joan, Mary, Betty, and Ruth."
Or:
"Yes, I like you. I like Mary *better, though.*"

Notice that this second sentence contains not one, but two Connectors. Both tie the two sentences together. One by comparison *(better)*. The other by contrast *(though)*.
Or:
"Yes, I like you. *But such* a feeling is so foreign to me that I'm frightened."

Here, again, we have two Connectors in the second sentence. *But,* showing contrast. And *such,* tying the Picture Word *feeling,* in the second sentence into the Picture Word *like* in the first sentence.

And so on. As we have seen, you have literally dozens of such linking Connectors as these to choose from, when you want to link any two sentences together. They are, indeed, our first type of sentence Connector.

But now we go on to a new type of Connecting Word. A second kind of sentence Connector. A kind of Connecting Word that you have not encountered before, which joins two sentences together in a different way.

This new kind of Connecting Word is not simply a way to link two word-pictures together, like the other Connecting Words we have already examined.

Instead, our second kind of Connecting Word does this: *It condenses the thought in the first sentence (or a part of that thought) into a single word, and then carries that condensed thought forward in the second sentence.*

This is why we call it a *condensing Connector.*
For example:
"The handsome young knight in shining white armor rode up to the castle. Then he imperiously knocked at the gate."

The condensation here is of the image *"The handsome young knight in shining white armor."* And in the second sentence this entire image is summarized in the condensing

Connector *he.*

Why is this done? Once again, to help your listener's mind understand your developing thought, as you carry it along from sentence to sentence.

As we said before, the human mind cannot hold too many words, or too many thoughts, in conscious focus at one time. Therefore, you should think of your listener's mind as a kind of movie screen, upon which you flash one thought, let her understand it, and then flash another.

But – since you do not want her to forget the first thought when you give her the second – you condense some part of that first thought into a single word, and include that condensing word in your second thought.

This is what we have done in the example above. We started out with a long and complicated word-picture, *The handsome young knight in the shining white armor.* We paused long enough at the end of this sentence to let our listener understand it.

And then – because she had understood it, because she did not therefore need it repeated in the second sentence, but instead wished to go on with the next thought – we condensed it into the single Connecting Word *he.* And then we let *he* be the actor in the next sentence.

This use of condensing Connectors is, as you can see, a marvelous way of developing your thought from one sentence to the next. It is especially powerful when you use it in conjunction with the road-sign words we have already explored in this chapter.

Let us therefore look at some more of these condensing Connectors, and how they enable us to carry forward the thought of whole sentences in a single word:

We have already used the condensing Connector *he,* which can carry forward the full description of any male actor in your first sentence. Now let's look at its partner *she,* which we use in this way:

"Then I was introduced to a tall, blond, infinitely beautiful creature named Rachael. Although I am sure that *she* had heard of me before, from Martin, *she* showed no sign of recognition, or of interest."

Here, the condensing Connector *she* is used twice in the second sentence, to bind that sentence firmly, in the listener's imagination, to the first. You can practically see the blond, beautiful face turning to meet the narrator, and feel his disappointment when she shows no sign of interest in him.

Notice, too, that we could have changed that second sentence slightly, to include still another condensing Connector in it. And thus bind it in a different way to the first. Like this:

"Then I was introduced to a tall, blond, infinitely beautiful creature named Rachael. Although I am sure that *she* had heard of me before, there was no sign of recognition, or of interest, in *her* eyes."

Once again, the image of the beautiful face is carried over from the first sentence to the second. And then evoked twice in that second sentence, without ever repeating the original description.

This is how you build a unified story out of a series of sentences. How you carry your listener along with you through a series of continually expanding images, that are yet perfectly connected together.

Now, of course, we can go from a single actor to a group of actors. And develop this expanding image:

"The corporal chose O'Hara, and Bernstein, and Marcello, and Washington. *Each* of *them* selected a rifle, a revolver, and twenty rounds of ammunition. And then *they* mounted *their* horses and slowly rode off toward the mountain."

I suggest that you study the four condensing Connectors used to tie these three sentences together. First, five men are pointed out to the listener in the first sentence. Then, in the second sentence, they are evoked again – first separately, by *each,* and then collectively, by *them.*

And then, in the third sentence, the listener is made to see all five of them mounting their horses and riding off by the condensing Connectors *they* and *their.*

This is far more efficient than trying to carry the image from sentence to sentence by mechanically repeating it.

For example, like this:

"The corporal chose O'Hara, and Bernstein, and Marcello, and Washington. The corporal and O'Hara and Bernstein and Marcello and Washington each selected a rifle, a revolver, and twenty rounds of ammunition. And then the corporal and O'Hara and Bernstein and Marcello and Washington mounted the corporal's horse and O'Hara's horse and Bernstein's horse and Marcello's horse and Washington's horse and slowly rode off toward the mountain."

No listener wants this kind of repetition. No listener's mind needs this kind of repetition. In fact, what it does is block the new Images you are trying to give him.

So, what you do when you write a stream of sentences is this:

1.   The first image, in its own sentence, must be developed as vividly as possible. *"Yesterday, I hit that miserable son-of-a-gun, Harry."*

2.   Then you condense at least part of that image – *that miserable son-of-a-gun, Harry* – into a condensing Connector – *him.*

3.   And then you make that condensing Connector a part of the image that you are developing in the next sentence. "And then I hit *him* again."

4.   And so on. "Until *he* fell to the ground, with *his* mouth bleeding." Sentence after sentence. "And then *he* looked up at me, and begged me not to hit *him* again." Until your listener has your full story.

Each step of the way, your sentences are connected. Your listener knows exactly how each one fits into the sentence before it.

And – notice again – that you have done this not only with condensing Connectors, but also in each sentence with linking Connectors: *"And then* I hit him again. *Until* he fell to the ground, with his mouth bleeding. *And then* he looked up at me and begged me not to hit him again."

Fortunately, our language is almost as full of these condensing Connectors as it is of the linking Connectors. Here are a few of the most important:

It. For example: "The table is genuine Chippendale. *It* cost us $3,000."

This. For example: "Follow this road for a mile, and then turn left at the first stoplight. *This* is by far the best way to get on the Turnpike."

(Notice that *this,* like many other Connectors, can serve double duty. It can simply be part of a sentence, as it is in "Follow *this* road." Or it can serve as a condensing Connector between two sentences, as it does in *"This* is by far the best way." It all depends on how you choose to use it.)

That. For example: "I am staying here. I will never move. And *that* is all there is to it."

These. For example: "You may leave on your own two feet. Or you will be carried out. *These* are your two choices."

Both. For example: "You may say, 'Jane and I will go to school tomorrow,' or 'Jane and I shall go to school tomorrow.' *Both* are correct."

One. For example: "There stands Macbeth on the brow of the hill, and there strides Macduff toward him. *One* shall not live till morning."

Which. For example: "But you still pleaded with him for my life. *Which* shows again how insane your love for me really is."

Such. For example: "He suffers from gout, diabetes, and perpetual indigestion. *Such,* my dear Watson, are the penalties of gluttony."

Notice, incidentally, that these condensing Connectors do not have to be used alone to link two sentences together. You may also join them with a Picture Word, to form a *linking phrase.* Like this:

"Next, you pick up the small wrench marked Number 16. Then you use *this wrench* to tighten each of the engine nuts, from left to right, in turn."

Or:

"You hold your dancing partner with your right hand firmly around her waist, and your left hand firmly in her right. *In this way,* you begin to lead her around the floor."

Notice also that this three-word phrase, *In this way,*

condenses the entire sentence in front of it: *"You hold your dancing partner with your right arm firmly around her waist, and your left hand firmly in her right."* And, by so doing, it allows the listener to put that entire sentence into this motion: *"you begin to lead her around the floor."* All without the slightest mental effort on her part.

So you have now seen two separate tasks that these condensing Connectors can perform for you:

1.   *To carry forward a part of a sentence.* And
2.   *To carry forward that entire sentence – or its core meaning – into the next sentence for you.*

And, as I have pointed out to you before (in the last *Harry* example, a few pages back), not only can they be used to carry a thought from one sentence to the next, but throughout a whole stream of sentences.

Here is an example of this continuing stream of connections:

"There is no doubt in my mind that this is *the best team the Yankees have had in years. They* have not only been completely rebuilt in the past five years, but *their* pitching can't be matched anywhere in the country today.

"And just look what happened to *them* in *their* first three games. Both Baltimore and Boston only managed to get two hits each from *them* in twenty-seven innings.

"And *they're* averaging six runs a game right now. Yes Sir, brother, *these* are the Yankees that are going to bring the pennant back to New York."

Now, this stream of sentences is rich in insights for you. Notice, first of all, that the starting image *(the best team the Yankees have had in years)* is carried by *they, their, them, they're,* and *these* through five additional sentences, without the slightest confusion.

In each of these additional sentences, more information is given the reader about *the best team the Yankees have had in years.* His understanding of them deepens with each sentence.

All this information could have never been loaded into one sentence. Such a sentence would simply have been incomprehensible. *So the main thought of that sentence was taken out of it, and spread across five additional sentences, where the necessary information could be fed to the reader step by step, with complete understanding.*

This is the process of *elaboration* – of *giving your reader (or listener) more and more information about a core-image as she goes from sentence to sentence.* It is only possible through the use of these condensing Connectors.

We will spend an entire chapter on elaboration later on. But this shows you now the enormous communication power these various types of Connectors immediately give you.

So we now have two types of sentence Connectors: We have Connecting Words that serve as links between sentences. And we have Connecting Words that serve as condensers, to carry thoughts from one sentence to another.

And we also have a third, and last, type of sentence Connector, which is not a word at all. This type of Connector is made up of all those punctuation marks, and sentence structures, that tell our reader how any two sentences fit together.

For example, there are two punctuation marks that can serve as sentence Connectors. They are:

The full colon. (For example, throughout this book, I have used this full-colon structure: *For example:)*

Or, to give another example, from earlier in this book:

"So we can combine both problems of understanding – and their solutions – into this simple rule:

"Always try to make each image complete, and do it in as few words as possible."

Notice, in both these examples, that the full colon works as an identity Connector. It tells your reader immediately that the sentence that follows it is identical with the sentence, or phrase, that preceded it.

Thus, in the second example, the full colon told your reader that *"this simple rule"* was identical with *"Always try to make each image complete …"* etc.

In fact, what you are doing with this full colon is signaling your reader, in advance, that your next sentence is going to be equal to part of your first. Thus, the full colon serves the same function, between sentences, as the identity Connecting Words (such as *is* or *are*) serve within each sentence.

Just as *is* or *are* tells you that two words are equal within a sentence *(Sally* is my *wife),* so the full colon tells you that two sentences are equal when it joins them together.

And, in the same way, when you use the second punctuation mark as a sentence Connector – the *question mark* – you also show identity.

Like this:

"And what does this tyrant wish from us? Our homes, our produce, our fields and our families!"

Here, the question mark tells your reader that *"What does this tyrant wish from us"* is identical to everything listed in the second sentence.

Thus, it is available, when you wish to use it, as another identity Connector between sentences.

So there we have the two punctuation marks that are used as sentence Connectors – the *full colon,* and the *question mark.* Notice that, until your attention is called to them, they are even less noticeable than our shy little Connecting Words.

And now we come to our final sentence Connectors, which are completely invisible, since they are simply the *sentence structure* itself. The way we *arrange* our words to show the connection between one sentence and the next.

The simplest of them is *repetition.* Here is an example of how it can be used to tie two sentences together:

"And at the end of this sentence, he sees *the same thing* that you do. He thinks *the same thing* that you do."

Here, the identical phrase, *the same thing,* is repeated twice in two sentences. By making this repetition, you have signaled the reader that your core thought – *the thought that you wish to carry over from one sentence to the next* – is contained in these three words.

And yet, at the same time, you have elaborated and developed this core thought as you moved it from the first sentence to the second. You have done this with the Picture Word *sees* in the first sentence. And then the Picture Word *thinks* in the second.

So you have led your reader from one aspect of your core thought to the next. But, at the same time, you have kept that core thought in his mind in both sentences through repetition.

Once again, this is the process of *elaboration – the planned development of your thought from sentence to sentence.* And we shall explore it more deeply in a later chapter.

So the first way we use the sentence structure itself to connect our sentences together is *repetition.*

The second is *sentence-structure expectation.* It is simply the fact, once again, that *your reader expects your sentence to take a certain form. And you can use that expectation – you can deliberately exploit it – to connect two or more sentences together so that she will immediately understand them.*

Here are some examples:

"If I understand her correctly, she must have had at least one lover before you. *Or two. Or three. Or four.*"

Here you have one long sentence, followed by three short ones. The three short sentences have no actor-word, and no action-word, and yet you understand them immediately. Why?

Because they exploit a thought-structure that is firmly imprinted on your mind: That one is followed by two. And then three. And then four.

It is this known thought-structure, this accepted numerical thought-structure, that allows these sentences to be separated – emphasized by their separation – and yet immediately understood.

Also, of course, the three later sentences are prepared for in the first sentence by the phrase *at least.* And each of them starts with the road-sign Connector *Or.*

So everything is laid out for the reader. He is tipped off in advance about what is coming. He is directed by a road–sign at each sentence-interval. And the numerical structure he has followed all his life is reinforced by the sequence and content of the four sentences.

He simply cannot go wrong. He understands immediately, effortlessly. And then is ready to go on.

Here is another example:

"Each one of these words carries a picture inside itself. That picture stands out by itself. You need no other words to support it. It is there. It exists. You can *see it. Smell it. Taste it. Touch it. Draw it. Show it on movie film.*"

Here, you exploit another expectation on the part of your reader: That of the normal sentence structure – actor ... action ... thing acted upon.

Thus, when you have given your reader a normal sentence *(You can see it),* and then repeat the last part of the structure of that sentence *(Smell it)* she will understand immediately that the actor *(You)* is the same in this second sentence.

And then you can go on to repeat that structure over and over again *(Taste it. Touch it. Draw it. Show it on movie film.)* And she will understand that all of these continuing sentences still have the same actor.

Your sentence Connections here are obtained entirely from her familiarity with the normal sentence structure. And therefore from her willingness to extend part of that structure over into a number of similar sentences.

This is an important insight. Because there are dozens of ways to use it. And because, as we shall see later, it gives you the key to making your sentences as simple as you want them to be.

Here is another example of how you use this extended sentence to connect a series of short and simple sentences:

"They tell us how Picture Words are connected to each other *in time. In space. In meaning. And in sequence.*"

Here, the last part of the first sentence depends on the Connecting Word *in.* So, not only is the structure of that part repeated in each succeeding sentence, but the Connecting Word is too. Thus, the reader is given two clues to make sure he can move effortlessly into each new sentence.

Also, because your reader is so familiar and so comfortable with the normal sentence structure, you don't even have to give it all to him in the first sentence. You can separate it into two sentences. And, if the connection is close enough, he will still understand you.

Like this:

"This is important. *For two reasons.*"

This thought, of course, could have been conveyed in one sentence. But, to gain greater emphasis, it is separated into two. And it still gains the same immediate understanding.

In addition, the structure in the second sentence does not even have to be similar to that in the first. It can actually be opposed to it – as long as that opposition is a common and accepted one. Like this:

"A sentence needs to have *only enough* words in it to be understood. *And no more. Only enough to be understood.*"

Here, you have exploited the commonly accepted opposition between *only enough* and *and no more*. By separating that opposition into two sentences, you have gained both simplicity and emphasis. And then you have reinforced that emphasis by your third sentence, which repeats the last part of the first sentence with a slight variation.

And so on. Once again, there are dozens of ways you can use structure to tie your sentences – and whole passages of sentences – together. We shall look at many of them in the chapters to come.

So there you have them all. All three ways of connecting your sentences together. They are, once again:

1.   The linking Connectors, which tell your reader how your thought-flow is linked together from one sentence to the next. Like: *and ... but ... however ... still ... because ... in fact ...* and all the rest.

2.   The condensing Connectors, which condense and carry your thought forward from one sentence to the next. Like: *he ... she ... it ... they ... that ... one ... both ... which ...* and all the rest.

3.   The non-word Connectors – the punctuation marks and sentence-structure expectations – that give you a third way, not only to carry your thought forward from sentence to sentence, but to tell your reader exactly in which direction it's going.

How do you use any and all of these Connectors? There is only one simple rule:

Each sentence after the first must have a Connector in it that links it up to the sentence before. And that Connector should be as close to the front of the second sentence as possible.

You can use anyone of the three types of Connectors you wish. Or you can use two or more of them. But each sentence you compose must have at least one of them in it.

These, then, are our tools. First among them are the Picture Words, which form the images we use to communicate with other people.

Then come the Connecting Words – and even Connectors that are not made of words – that enable us to join these Picture Words into immediately understandable sentences. And then enable us to join these sentences into whole stories, or reports, or textbooks, or poems.

Throughout this entire process, our goal is to be understood. To transmit the thoughts and images in our minds into other people's minds. And to do it as vividly and clearly as possible.

We now have the first rules we need to do this. Rules that have taught us how to link two sentences together in complete understanding. Now we will go on, and learn how to write as clearly and as simply as we wish. Or, if we wish, how to write with symbolism or metaphor or wit. And how to gain emphasis and power in our writing, and avoid monotony.

But first, always, with every sentence that we write, we must be understood.

The rest of the book gives you these guidelines. You provide the images; I try to give you the best way to get them across.

Exercises and Applications
for Chapter 4

In this chapter, you have gained two vital new tools: First, a new use for the linking Connectors. How to use them to link together two sentences, just as you have already used them to link together two word-pictures.

This is merely an extension of what you have learned before. The same rules and techniques apply. In fact, you have already practiced this kind of sentence-linking in the exercises for Chapter 2.

So you need no further practice with them here. For each exercise, either fill in the blank line or circle the correct word or phrase.

We can assume that you already know what these linking Connectors are, and how you use them to join together your sentences.

So we'll go on now to the new Connectors that you have not used before. The first of these is the condensing Connectors.

1.   As you know, a condensing Connector takes a thought from one sentence, condenses that _____ into a single word, and then uses that word as a part of the next sentence.

This is terribly important, because we cannot retain too many fully stated thoughts in our minds at one time. Therefore, we have to condense them continually. And use these condensing Connectors to carry forward our core thought into wider and wider elaborations of that thought.

2.   So we understand the full core thought in the first sentence. And then we *(condense/expand)* it into a single word in the second sentence. And use that word to carry it forward, and learn more about it, from that moment on.

3.   Now, our first task in learning to use a new kind of word is simply to see it. If we can't see it, we can't use it.

So let's take a series of double-sentences right now, and find out what kinds of thoughts we can condense into a single word.

For example:

I met my first German today. He tells me many interesting secrets."

What is the condensing Connector used in the second sentence? _____

4.   What part of the first sentence does it condense?

_____

_____

5.   Your answer might be *my first German* (which is the answer I've left the blanks for). Or it may simply be *German*. I like the first answer. But the second answer is not wrong, just (to my way of thinking) a little incomplete.

But the first part of the question, *What is the condensing Connector* has only one answer. It has to be *he*.

So we now have an example of a condensing Connector that carries along part of the sentence in front of it. Here's another one:

"Grant and McNeill had long since learned to regulate their lives. They moved and thought now with grace and beauty. "

What is the condensing Connector in the second sentence? _____

6.   What part of the first sentence does it condense?

_____

_____

Here, the two main actors in a story are introduced in its first sentence. And then are carried along in the next sentence (and in many more sentences) by the condensing Connector *they*.

7.   Now take this example:

"He had planned to wait a hundred years. More than that he dared not delay. "

What is the condensing Connector in the second sentence? _____

8.   What part of the first sentence does it condense?

_____

(Notice that any part of a sentence, beginning, or middle, or end, can be carried along into the next sentence by the condensing Connector.)

Notice, also, that two condensing Connectors are used here. *He,* in the second sentence, which carries forth the condensing Connector *He,* of the first sentence. And *more than that,* which condenses a hundred years.

9.   Now, as we have seen, the same condensing Connector can be used to carry the original image along, not through just one more sentence, but through several.

Here's how this was done in the continuation of our first example:

"I met my first German today. He tells me many interesting secrets. He was in Hitler's army. Then he escaped to Argentina, then to the U.S.A. He has volunteered in the American Army because in this way he can kill more Communists and become an American citizen."

Here is a stream of five sentences, all linked by the condensing Connector _____.

10.   By using this condensing Connector, the original image, _____ _____ _____, is carried through all five sentences, without having to be repeated each time.

Notice that you still, automatically, retain the original image in each succeeding sentence. You still know that it's the German who's the actor in each one of these sentences.

But it is an incredible convenience not to have to repeat that original image every time you want to use it in a new sentence. Let's see just how tedious that would be.

11.   Here is the same stream of sentences. This time, however, you write in the original image in each succeeding sentence:

"I met my first German today. _____ tells me many interesting secrets. _____ was in Hitler's army. Then _____ escaped to Argentina, then to the U.S.A. _____ has

volunteered in the American Army because in this way
_____ *can kill more Communists and become an*
American citizen."

What work! And this is a brief example, because I wanted to spare both of us. How much easier it is simply to roll up this whole image into a single word, *he,* and use that to carry it along from that point on.

12.   And this is especially important when you carry along, not just part of the first sentence, but the entire sentence itself.

For example:

"I believe in the existence of a God who watches over us, protects us, and makes us all happy. And that's inborn, in my blood."

What is the condensing Connector in the second sentence? _____

13.   What is the thought (really, the entire first sentence) that it condenses?

_____

_____

Can you imagine trying to repeat that entire first sentence as part of the second sentence! The second sentence would then be so long, and so complicated, that it just couldn't be understood.

And this is why condensation – the ability to condense whole thoughts, and carry them forward from that moment on in a single word – is such a powerful characteristic of language.

In fact, without this characteristic, we really couldn't communicate with each other at all. We'd never be able to escape from our first thought. We'd never be able to develop a stream of thoughts, each one of which elaborates the one in front of it.

We'll explore some other benefits of condensation later in this exercise. Right now, however, let's go on with the two kinds of condensations that our condensing Connectors can give us.

14.   The first is the ability to condense part of the preceding sentence. And the second is the ability to condense that entire preceding sentence as a whole.

Here is another example of that second ability:

"I will give you $100,000 down, and $10,000 a month for six months thereafter. But this is my final offer."

What is the condensing Connector used in the second sentence? _____

15.   What is the thought it condenses?

_____

_____

16.   Now, what are the condensing Connectors we have available to carry thoughts like these forward? Let's examine each of them in turn.

Let's start with *he*. When you talk about a man in your first sentence, and wish to carry his image forward in subsequent sentences, the first condensing Connector you have to do so is *he*.

So write a description of a friend of yours in the first sentence here (Like, *"John is a rugged, six-foot-two-inch tall Irishman, who looks like he was carved out of a block of granite."*) And then condense that image into the actor of your second sentence, by using *he*. (Like, *"But he loves flowers, and grows the most beautiful orchids I've ever seen."*)

_____

_____

17.   All right. But it isn't necessary, of course, to make that condensation the actor of the second sentence. It can appear anywhere in that sentence at all. And if it's the person acted upon, then we use the condensing Connector *him*.

So write a third sentence now, using *him:*

_____

_____

18.   And, in another sentence, if you want to show possession, you use still another condensing Connector, *his.*
   Write a fourth sentence here, using *his:*

---

19.   So, that exhausts our male condensing Connectors.
Now, how about the females? You know all of them too, of
course. If a female is going to be the actor in the second
sentence, you use *she.*
   Write your first sentence, and then your second, *she,*
sentence here:

---

20.   Now, if *she's* going to be acted upon in that second
sentence, we use *her.* Write your *her* sentence here:

---

21.   And if we want to show possession, we write *hers.*
Write your *hers* sentence here:

---

22.   Which takes care of our female friends. Now, how
about animals, things, and ideas? We can carry forward
each one of those by the condensing Connector *it.*
   Write your first sentence, and then your second using *it*
as the actor, here:

---

23.   Now, if the animal, thing, or idea is acted upon in
that second sentence, we still use the same condensing
Connector, *it.* In this case, for some obscure reason, it
doesn't change.

So write another it sentence – but this time with *it* acted upon – here:

_____

_____

24. And, to show possession, we use *its*. Write your *its* sentence here:

_____

_____

25.   I know this is all perfectly simple, and that you know all of it already. But that's the beautiful part of it: Our language has already taught us, automatically, 99% of what we need to know to communicate correctly.

All we have to do is make ourselves a little more aware of these tools, which we've already used every day of our lives. And then we can put them to work again, with far greater control.

Let's go on to the plural condensing Connectors. The ones that allow us to carry forward the image of more than one person, place, thing, animal, idea, or what have you.

The first of them is *they*. It is used as the actor of the second sentence.

So write your first sentence, and then your second sentence using *they,* here:

_____

_____

26.   To show that *they* have been acted upon, we use, of course, *them*. So write a *them* sentence here:

_____

_____

27.   To show possession, we use *their,* or *theirs.* You already know where each goes. So write a *their* or *theirs* sentence here:

———————————————————————————

———————————————————————————

28.   We can also point out our plural Picture Words in our second sentence. In this case, we use *these.* (For example: "I like pickles and malted milkshakes. But *these* are the worst foods in the world for me.")
So write your *these* sentence here:

———————————————————————————

———————————————————————————

29.   Or, we can use *those.* Write your *those* sentence here:

———————————————————————————

———————————————————————————

So now we've reviewed our condensing Connectors for persons, places, things, ideas, animals, etc. Most of them, as you can immediately see, carry forth part of the sentence that precedes them.
30.   But what condensing Connectors do we have if we wish to carry forth all of the preceding sentence? Let's review them now.
The first of them is *this.* For example: "The United States of America is the greatest country in the world. I believe *this* with all my heart and soul."
So write a first sentence, and then a *this* sentence here:

———————————————————————————

———————————————————————————

31.   Then we have that. It works the same way as *this.* So let's see your *that* sentence here:

———————————————————————————

———————————————————————————

32.   And, as we saw in Chapter 4 itself, you may also use *both* in this way. Write your two *both* sentences here:

_____

_____

33.   You may also use *it* in this way. Write your first sentence, and then your *it* sentence here:

_____

_____

34.   You may also use *these* to carry forth the full sentence preceding it. Write your two *these* sentences here:

_____

_____

35.   And you may use *those*. Write your two *those* sentences here:

_____

_____

Now, this by no means exhausts all the condensing Connectors available to you. We have touched, for example, on *one* or *which,* both of which are given to you in Chapter 4.
36.   But, by now, you do get the idea. You do see that an entire image, composed of many words, in one sentence can be condensed into one *(word/sentence)* in the next sentence.
37.   And that single word in that second sentence can carry that image forward in all its original power.

No wonder we call these power-packed little words the _____ Connectors.
38.   And we have also reviewed the most important of them. You have used each of them to write your own condensing sentences. And they are now consciously and deliberately available to you, to condense your thoughts and carry them forward whenever you want to share them with another person.

You now have the principle of language condensation as an available tool to you. I think, however, that we should sidetrack here for a moment, and discuss another use of that principle that may also be of great value to you.

As we have seen before, the human mind cannot hold too many images in it at one time. It cannot hold too many words. And it cannot hold too many thoughts at one time.

This is a profound limitation. A limitation that has kept every other animal except humans under the control of nature, rather than the controller of nature.

Language is the tool humans have invented to overcome this limitation. Language first allows us to convert thoughts into words, and therefore store them. And language then allows us to condense these thoughts, and thus elaborate them into entire discourses.

And these logical and progressive discourses enable us to work out complicated paths of action. Actions that direct nature, and borrow its powers for our purposes.

We have already seen the first step in this process of condensation: The ability to take an image from one sentence, and carry it forward in a single word in the next sentence.

But there is also a second step that I want you to become aware of. And that is the combination of the process of definition with the process of condensation.

Definition, as we have seen, is the process of explaining a new word in terms of old words. Thus one word, which is new to your reader in terms of old words, is identified with a whole group of older words, all of which, however, are already familiar.

This is the basic step in definition. But it is only the first step.

What you have done when you have defined something is this: *You have made one new word take the place of many old ones.* Thus, you have condensed many old words into one new one.

And this new word is now available to your reader, to carry the whole idea it contains into a whole series of new sentences and new thoughts.

Thus this new word is *condensed wisdom.* It can carry

an entire complex idea around in it in as little as four letters. You can fit that newly condensed idea into a whole
series of brand new sentences – brand-new relationships –
brand-new ideas. And you can make that idea work for you
in ways that would have been impossible if you had to use
all of its previous old words to carry it along.

So *definition is the process of exchanging many old words
for one new word.* And condensation works from that point
on by allowing that one new word to relate that condensed
idea to a whole series of other ideas.

Language grows that way. Wisdom grows that way. Civilization grows that way.

It's a powerful process, and I think we should put it to
work on a trial basis right now.

39.   Let's see how a new definition of an everyday word
opens up a whole new world of meaning to us. As just one
example, some religions define *justice* as *protection for
society's victims.* As you can see, this is not at all like the
usual definition, which is *punishment for wrongdoing.*

This definition-shift could provide hours of fruitful
discussion for us. For example, we could say:

*"Justice is not, _____ as we've thought, but
protection for society's victims.*

40.   Then we could carry on the discussion further, by
saying: *"This means that _____ is not done in courts, by
judges and juries, but in the streets, by those who will risk
themselves to help others."*

Do you see how the whole new definition is carried
forward in that single old word? How you are using one
word to represent an entire new idea? And how this allows
you to pack thought into smaller and more usable packages
each time you do so?

41.   Now, the next time you encounter another new word,
write its definition here:

_____

_____

42. Now, use that new definition-word in a new sentence, to combine it with another idea:

_____

_____

Now, and this may be a little hard, can you use that new definition-word of yours as part of another definition, for another new word?

Let me give you an example: Let's say that you've been studying psychology. And you come across *id.* And you define it as *the basic, unconscious mass of life instincts.*

43. So you use *id* in sentence after sentence, until it becomes an automatic part of your vocabulary. Try one of these sentences here (for example, "I spend most of my life serving the needs of my *id,* and not my adult self."):

_____

_____

And now you go on with your study of psychology. And you encounter the term *super-ego.* And you define it as *that part of the id that serves as a person's unconscious moral judge.*

So you have used your first definition-word as a part of your second definition. Once again, you are continuing to condense complicated ideas into smaller and smaller packages. Each of which becomes easier and easier to use.

Any field of study, such as science, is first of all a collection of such definition-words. When you study the science, therefore, you first learn the definition-words. And then you learn the rules for putting them to work.

The more condensed the definition-words (i.e., one word contains several layers of condensed definitions within it), the more mature and more powerful the science. And the more you can do with any one of its terms.

So *definition* and *condensation* are two of the most powerful tools language can give you.

So we have now looked at the condensing Connectors, and how they work. And how condensation can provide us with a second powerful tool to share our thoughts with others.

Now let's go on to our third type of sentence Connector: The no-word Connector.

44.   The first of these, as you remember, was the *full colon.* So let's put it to work. Write two *full-colon* sentences here:

---

45.   The second punctuation-mark Connector is the *question mark.* Write two *question-mark* sentences here:

---

46.   So those are our two punctuation-mark Connectors. Now we go beyond them to our sentence structure Connectors, where we use the sentence structure itself to link together our sentences in an immediately apparent relationship.

The first of these is *repetition.* You've seen an example of how it's used on page 95. Now use it yourself here:

Next is *sentence-structure expectation.* There are several ways to use this. Let's briefly review each one.

We can use *numerical expectation* as we did on page 95. But this structure is rather limited. And your example would have to follow mine too closely to ask you to do it here.

So let's pass on to our next structure: *Normal sentence structure expectation,* with all its variations. Here the opportunities are wide open.

47.   First of all, you can vary the action Picture Words of the first sentence in the sentences that follow it, as we did on page 96.

Write your own version of this structure-linking mechanism here:

---

48.   Next, we can take the last connecting phrase in the first sentence, and vary it in the sentences that follow, as we did with *in* on page 97.
    Write your version here:

_____

_____

49.   Or, we can interrupt the normal sentence-structure expectation, and give it to our reader in two sentences instead of one. We saw an example of this on page 97.
    Now write your own version here:

_____

_____

    Now, in your two examples, did you use the same two Connecting Words that I did in mine – *in* and *for?* There was no need to do so, of course. You could have used other Connecting Words: *Of ... from ... to ... on ... and ...* and dozens more.
50.   Let's run quickly through some of them now. Write a sentence whose last connecting phrase begins with *to.* And then write a series of sentences connected to the first by a series of variations on that *to* phrase:

_____

_____

51.   Now write an interrupted sentence (changing it into two smaller sentences for the purpose of simplicity and emphasis), revolving around the Connecting Word *on:*

_____

_____

    And you could go on and on, of course. The possibilities are enormous. We will explore more of them in the next chapter, when we see how to make our sentences any length we desire.

52.   So there we have our three types of Connectors. The first are the linking Connectors, which tell your reader how your thought-flow is *(interrupted/linked)* together from one sentence to the next.

53.   The second are the condensing Connectors, which _____ a thought from one sentence down to one word, and then carry it forward in the next sentence.

54.   And the last are the non-word Connectors. First, the two punctuation marks: the full colon, and the *(comma/ question mark)*.

55.   And then the sentence-structure Connectors, which show how two sentences are connected by the use of the *(word-content/sentence-structure)* itself.

56.   Three types of Connectors. Hundreds of individual words and symbols in all. But they all follow one simple rule:

Every sentence after the first must have a _____ in it that links it up to the sentence before.

57.   And that Connector should be as close to the _____ of that second sentence as possible.

That's all you need. It is our basic operating rule. The rest is application.

And it is to that application that we turn now.

Chapter 5

How to Choose
the Right Length
for Your Sentences

So WE HAVE our pictures and our Connectors. And we want to put them together in a series of understandable and related thoughts for our reader.

We call these complete and immediately understandable units of thought sentences. In Chapter 2, we defined *a sentence* as this:

As much of your thought as you choose to give the other person at one time. So that he can understand this part of your thought the moment he hears it. And then pass on to the next.

We have already seen how to construct each of these sentences by itself, in Chapter 3. And then, in Chapter 4, we looked at the between-sentence Connectors, which made sure that your reader could pass from one sentence to the next without confusion.

Now, in this chapter, we are going to see how each sentence fits into the *total flow* of your thought. And how an awareness of this thought-flow can enable you to adjust the length of your sentences to give you as much simplicity, clearness, and emphasis as you want.

The key, here, is this:

That each of your sentences only has to be understood at the particular moment you speak or write it.

In other words, it has to have meaning – it has to make sense – only within the flow of your thought at that very moment. And not at any other time.

Let me give you an example. Do you think that the following is a sentence:

"None."

Probably you' d say no. Why? Because it doesn't make sense. It is not immediately understandable the moment the reader encounters it.

And you are right – since it was just sitting there on the page by itself.

But what would happen if we put it into a flow of thought? Like this:

"How many people paid $100 per ticket?"

"None."

Now it makes sense. Perfect sense.

Why? Because the flow of thought has given it meaning that it didn't have when it stood alone.

This is important for two reasons:

1.   Because it shows again that no sentence is ever used alone. It's always used with other sentences, as part of a flow of thought.

And

2.   Because it shows that a sentence can get much of its meaning from the sentence in front of it.

In fact, it can get as much meaning from the preceding sentence as it does from its own words within it.

So our next Operating Rule is this:

Each of your sentences needs to have only enough words in it to be understood in the flow of your thought. And no more. Only enough to be understood.

This means that a good sentence, a working sentence, an effective sentence, need only have one word.

It can be as simple as *"Yes."* Or *"No."* *"Up."* Or *"Down."*

It all depends on the sentence that came before it. On the way your flow of thought is developing.

If that preceding sentence sets up the new sentence's meaning, then that new sentence need have only one word.

Or two. Or three. Or four.

Look at the sentences in this chapter. Many of them have fewer than three or four words. But you have probably understood them all.

Many of them have not even had a single actor-word, or action-word.

But you still understood them. Because they made sense in the thought-flow of this chapter.

So now we know that *a sentence needs only enough words in it to be understood.* And understood at the particular moment that the reader encounters it.

And that some sentences get most of their meaning from the sentence that comes before them. Rather than from their own words.

So we can make our sentences any length we choose. From one word to dozens of words. Any number is right.

All a good sentence has to do is be understood. And all the words it needs are enough words to be understood.

So, *if we feel a sentence is too long to be clear, we can break it up.* We can make two or more sentences out of it.

And – if we put in the right Connecting Words, and the right sentence-structure explanation – we can build as much clarity into those sentences as we need.

This is why it's so valuable to know that we can make our sentences as long, or as short, as we choose.

Because this gives us the tool we need to build variety and clarity and emphasis into our flow of thought.

Once again, then, our basic operating rules are these:

1.   *Each of your sentences needs to have only enough words in it to be understood in the flow of your thought.*

2.   *Each sentence after the first, no matter how long or how short, must have a Connector that links it up to that flow of thought, as it is developing in the sentence before.*

(Although, as we saw in the last chapter, that Connector need be nothing more than an invisible sentence-structure expectation.)

These, then, are our rules. Now let's put them to work to develop our flow of thought ...

**Exercises and Applications
for Chapter 5**

In the following exercises, either circle the correct choice, or fill in the blank line.

This chapter dealt with the art of the short sentence. It showed you how to make your sentences as short as you wish by following these two rules:

1. Each of your sentences needs to have only enough words in it to be *(understood/rephrased)* in the flow of your thought.

2. And each sentence after the first, no matter how long or how short, must have a _____ that links it up to that flow of thought, as it was developed in the sentence before.

These two rules are quite simple. And, even better, they come right out of the rules you've already learned. So you can put them to work at once.

Now, you don't want to make all your sentences short. But, when you need a short sentence – to punch home a point, or make it perfectly clear – you want to be able to construct one automatically.

So the exercises I give you here are designed for one purpose: To make you familiar with the use of short sentences. And the many different ways you can build them into your thought-flow. So they're available to you when you want them.

To do this, I'm going to show you various opportunities, in your ordinary thought flow, that you can turn into short sentences.

We've already started this, in the last set of exercises, when we dealt with sentence-structures as a kind of Connector.

Now let's go on. Here are some other opportunities: I'll name the pattern first, in italics, and then show you how to reproduce it.

3. *Commentary.* For example:
    "You are a beautiful girl. I mean it."

The pattern here: Say something. Then comment on it.
Try one yourself here:

---

4.   *Set-Apart Cause.* For example:
"There is no car like a Volvo. Because it never grows old."
The pattern here: State a fact, then give your reason in the next sentence. (You can give more than one, of course, if you wish. And you can put them each, in a separate sentence.)
Write your version here:

---

5.   *Set-Apart Detail.* For example:
"So I hit him with a bottle. Hard on his head."
The pattern here: First the main word-picture. Then an isolated detail.
Write your version here:

---

6.   *Set-Apart Time.* For example:
"I have always been fascinated by the English. Since the very beginning."
The pattern here: State the event. Then specify how long it exists – or has existed – in time.
Write your version here:

---

7.   *Set-Apart Reason.* For example:
"I like French-speaking people. They pay well. They seldom insult. They give me a chance to improve my French."

The pattern here: State a fact. Give your reasons. (Same as exercise 3 above, but here the Connecting Word, *because,* is dropped. The sentence structure itself provides the connection.)

Write your version here:

_____

_____

8.   *Set-Apart Contrast.* For example:
"It was a messy life. But very instructive."

The pattern here: State a fact. Contradict it in the next sentence. Let your reader wait till the third sentence to realize how the two fit together.

Write your version here:

_____

_____

9.   *Split-Up Action.* For example:
"I accept reality. I face it."

The pattern here: Take a complicated action (with more than two parts). State the first part in one sentence. And the second in the next sentence.

This pattern is a variation of exercise 46 in the last chapter. But there we dropped the actor after the first sentence.

Here we keep him in the second sentence.

You can do it either way. Write your version here:

_____

_____

10.   *Expanded-Repetition.* For example:
"They gave me lessons about religion, hygiene, behavior, sex. Even sex."

The pattern here: If a point in the first sentence is important enough, repeat it. But, this time, emphasize, comment, or expand on it.

Write your version here:

_____

_____

11.   *Set-Apart Definition.* For example:

"I adore Doctor Williams. My second father, my teacher, my everything."

The pattern here: Name something or someone in the first sentence. Identify him in the second with or without an identity Connector.

Write your version here:

_____

_____

12.   *Set-Apart Sequence.* For example:

"The Reverend will introduce the two of us. There will be a shy meeting and a short bow the first time.

Then a second meeting in the church.

Then many dates in the church.

Then, he'll touch my hand."

The pattern here: Start an action sequence in the first sentence. Then present fragments of the developing sequence of events in succeeding sentences, with the time structure as the Connector. Try to lead to a climax, as in the last sentence above.

Write your own version here:

_____

_____

13.   *Repeated Action.* For example:

"Paris fell. Henry wept. I wept. My father wept."

The pattern here: In the first (or, in this case, second) sentence, set up an action. In succeeding sentences, shift it from one actor, to another, to another.

Write your version here:

_____

_____

And so on. There are many more such patterns, of course. You might keep an inventory of them. Some have narrow application, such as the *repeated action* above.

Others have almost infinite application, such as the *set-apart detail*. For example, here are two other ways it can be used:

"He kept avoiding my lips. Still shy, respectful, holy."

Or:

"I felt her slow pulse. Still slow and erratic.

Very slow.

Too slow."

Notice, in this second example, how the drama grows by the use of nothing more than added details to the Picture Word *slow*.

Here, a detail *(slow)* is first set apart from the original sentence, and then elaborated or expanded upon. So two patterns (4 and 9 above) are used here to reinforce one another. To gain an even stronger effect.

14. Try this yourself. Take any two of the patterns you've learned here. And weave them together in one developing sequence:

———————————————————————————

———————————————————————————

Now, two words of caution:

First, the real reason you learn how to write short sentences is this: Because, as you'll see in the next chapter, short sentences are simple sentences. And simple sentences are easily understood.

Once again, your primary goal is always to be immediately understood. You want your reader to understand every sentence you write.

And when your ideas are complicated (have many elements), or difficult (are unfamiliar to your reader), then you have to shorten your sentences to make sure she understands their every step.

You do not use these short sentences because you prefer them over longer sentences. It is not a matter of taste at all. It is a matter of efficiency. Of being understood.

And the next chapter will explain to you, in detail, how these short sentences help you be understood.

And, as a final caution, you don't want to write too many short sentences, one after another, anyway. If you did, your writing would be too choppy. And too boring.

So you want to save these short sentences for the rough points in your discourse. For the hard thoughts. For the important ideas that you want to slam home.

And you want to mix them up with longer sentences for the easy stretches.

This technique – of building variety into your sentence-flow – will be shown to you in Chapter 7.

But right now, let's turn back to the text itself. And learn the simple art of simplicity ...

Chapter 6

How to Write Simply — So That Anyone Can Understand Your Most Complicated Thoughts

Y OU ARE NOW ready to tell other people your ideas. You are about to pick up a pencil, or start to speak, and transfer your thoughts into their minds.

Once again, you do this through words and sentences. Through images and Connectors. Till you have taken an entire flow of thought as complicated as a novel, for example, and conveyed it, intact, from your mind to another's.

And, once again, you have a single continuing goal: To be understood every step of the way. So that you never confuse or lose your reader. So that she follows you effortlessly from beginning to end.

To do this, you want to build certain characteristics into your writing. They are:

- You want it to be *simple,* so that your reader understands every step in your thought, before you take her on to the next.
- You want it to be *clear,* so that your reader doesn't think that you're saying one thing, when you're really saying another.
- You want it to be *predictable,* so that your reader is prepared for a new thought before she encounters it.

125

So that your train of thought develops the way she expects it to develop.

- And you want it to be *complete,* so that you have said everything you have wanted to say, in exactly the right place.

Let us now devote one chapter to each of these characteristics, and see how to build each of them into your train of thought.

The first is *simplicity.* The art of writing simply, so that your reader understands every step in your thought, before you take him on to the next.

We already have the two keys to simplicity. They are:

1.   The various Connectors that show your reader exactly how your Pictures (or ideas) fit together.

And

2.   The ability to make your sentences shorter or longer, depending on whether you need more or less simplicity.

Therefore, the basic rule of writing simply is this:

To write simply, build a sentence that states that thought in the fewest possible words, and with the greatest number of Connectors.

Or, to put it another way:

Simplicity is a ratio between the total number of words in a sentence and the number of Connecting Words in it. The higher the number of Connecting Words to total words in that sentence, the simpler it is.

Or, to put it another way:

To make an idea more simple, break it up into a number of short sentences. And use as many Connectors as possible to link up those sentences.

Let's see how this idea works. Let's take some complicated ideas and make them simple.

Here's one from a book of children's stories:

"They all stood fascinated forming a wall around the bucket where the drops of water were producing ripples that would move from the center to the edge one after another."

And here's how we'd simplify it. The first step is simply to pick out all the images in it, and number them, like this:

"(1) They all stood fascinated ... (2) forming a wall around the bucket ... (3) where the drops of water were producing ripples ... (4) that would move from the center to the edge one after another."

Now, after we've separated our images, we check each one of them to see if it's clear as it stands.

If it is clear, we leave it alone. If it's not clear, we simplify it by adding Connectors, and then putting each basic image, into a separate sentence of its own.

And we come up with something like this:

"They all stood fascinated, *and* formed a wall around the bucket. *In the bucket,* the drops of water were producing ripples. *These ripples* would move from the center *of the bucket* to the edge, one after another."

I have italicized the new Connectors for you. I have also numbered each new simplification, to correspond with the similar image in the original sentence.

Now let's see how each of these simplifications was created:

Simplification 1. It will help if you look at the story told in the original sentence as if you saw it through a movie camera. Your first shot, therefore, is a long shot, showing the children standing around the bucket. This long shot should be your first revised sentence.

The first thing your reader sees in this long shot is the first image of the original sentence. *They all stood fascinated.*

This image is perfectly clear as it stands. So we leave it as it is, and go on to the next one:

Simplification 2. The second image, *forming a wall around the bucket,* is not quite clear enough yet.

Why? Because a Connector between these first two images is missing. So I have added the Connector *and.* And then, to give even a stronger tie-in between the two word-pictures, I have changed *forming* to *formed,* to make its ending fit in with *stood.*

And then I ended the first sentence. So that it now contains these two parallel actions:

"They all *stood* fascinated, and *formed* a wall around the bucket."

The action is now perfectly clear throughout the entire sentence. It shows the reader all we want her to see from far away.

Simplification 3. Now we go on to the third original word picture: *Where the drops of water were producing ripples.*

This is the beginning of our close-up shot. We are now through with our long shot, and – beginning with these words – we bring our reader up close to see what happens in the bucket.

But, to make this shift from long shot to close-up, we have to give our reader a bridge. A connecting bridge between what she sees far away, and what she sees close up.

The original sentence tries to provide this bridge with the Connector *where.* But it is not strong enough, because it is not visual enough.

So we make it stronger by naming, once again, the place in which the close-up action occurred. We thus start our second sentence with the phrase *In the bucket ...*

And then we go on to show our reader the first step of what was happening in that bucket: *The drops of water were producing ripples.*

And so our second revised sentence reads:

"In the bucket, the drops of water were producing ripples."

Now the shift from long shot to close-up is perfectly clear.

And so is the first step of what was happening in the bucket.

Simplification 4. Notice that we showed our reader only this first step. When we were through with this first step, we stopped the sentence.

Compare this with the old close-up sentence (word-pictures 3 and 4), which went like this:

"...where the drops of water were producing ripples that would move from the center to the edge one after another."

Why the difference between this original version, and our shorter sentence? Why do we stop at the end of the first step?

Because what was happening in that bucket was just too complicated a process to be given to the reader at one time. To be given to him in one picture, in one sentence.

Therefore, the simplest way to present this process (as

it is to present any complicated process) is to break it up into several steps. And feed each step to your reader in a separate sentence.

This is what we have done. We have taken the first step – *where the drops of water were producing ripples* – and have given it its own sentence: *In the bucket, the drops of water were producing ripples.*

And now we are going to take the next step – *that would move from the center to the edge one after another* – and we are going to let it, too, have its own sentence.

How do we do this? In the same way we constructed the first-step sentence before it.

There, we started the sentence with the phrase *In the bucket.*

We used that phrase as a connecting bridge to the sentence in front of it *(They all stood fascinated, and formed a wall around the bucket),* by repeating the Picture Word *bucket* in both sentences.

And in this new sentence, we are going to do the same thing. We are going to take the Picture Word *ripples* from our second sentence, and we are going to start our new sentence with it.

Like this:

"These ripples would move ..."

So we now have this almost-complete thought sequence:

"They all stood fascinated, and formed a wall around the *bucket.* In the *bucket,* the drops of water were producing *ripples.* These *ripples* would move ..."

(Notice the two Picture Words repeated from sentence to sentence that were not in the original version. I have italicized them for you.)

But there is still one more detail to clarify. We still have to tell our reader exactly where the ripples are going to move.

The old version does not do this sharply enough. As you remember, it gave the reader only this information:

" ...would move from the center to the edge one after another."

But this image is still slightly blurred. It still leaves the reader with the question: "Move from the center to the edge of what?"

So we add *of the bucket.* And get:

"...would move from the center *of the bucket* to the edge, one after another."

And now our reader sees a complete word-picture. A sharp word-picture. And there can be no misunderstanding.

So that's it. A complete simplification procedure. Done by:

1.   *Separating overcrowded word-pictures into smaller, and therefore instantly understandable, units.*

And

2.   *Connecting these new sentence-units together with all the Connecting Words, and all the reinforcing Picture Words, they need.*

Of course, we don't want to write overloaded sentences in the first place. The whole goal of this book is to get you to write simple, understandable sentences from the very start.

But there is always a tendency, in all of us, to try to crowd too much into our sentences. We do it without noticing it.

And we do it at one point in our sentences especially. And I think we should pause now, and examine that "Overload Point," so we can help to avoid it in the future.

As you have seen in the example above, there is a tendency in all of us to overload certain Picture Words. The rule for detecting this overloading is simple:

We overload a Picture Word when we try to make it part of two word-pictures at once.

Just look at the original sentence again:

"They all stood fascinated forming a wall around the *bucket* where the drops of water were producing *ripples* that would move from the center to the edge one after another."

Here I have italicized the two overloaded Picture Words for you. Can you detect the feeling of "breathlessness" they give the sentence? A feeling of somehow running too far without stopping, and exhausting both your own breath and your listener's mind?

Let's see how each one of them, in its turn, causes this feeling of breathlessness:

The first of them, *bucket,* is used here as part of two word-pictures: *Forming a wall around the bucket...* and *(the bucket) where the drops of water were producing ripples.*

But it can't do both of these jobs at once. The shift from one word-picture to another is just too fast, and too poorly marked out by Connectors for the reader to be comfortable with it. Thus, the breathlessness.

And so, we've stopped the sentence at the end of the first word-picture. And then repeated *In the bucket* to start our new thought.

And so we have:

"They all stood fascinated, and formed a wall around the bucket. In the bucket, the drops of water were producing ripples."

But *ripples* is the second overloaded Picture Word. In the original version, it is used as part of these two word-pictures: *Where the drops of water were producing ripples ... and (ripples) that would move from the center to the edge one after another.* And therefore, our second point of misunderstanding occurs.

So we stop our second sentence after *ripples.* And we repeat *These ripples* again to start our third sentence.

So we have:

"In the bucket, the drops of water were producing ripples. These ripples would move from the center of the bucket to the edge one after another."

Do you see what we're doing here? We are simplifying by repeating. We are taking overloaded Picture Words and "unloading" them by using them twice, in two different sentences.

Over and over again, we are using *repetition* as a connecting and simplifying device. But we are strengthening and clearly marking that repetition with the proper Connecting Words *(In* and *These),* to make sure the reader knows exactly how they fit.

So let's repeat our troubleshooter rule again:

If you try to make a Picture Word serve as part of two images at once, you're in trouble.

Or, to phrase it differently:

If you find that you've written a confusing sentence, first find out whether you've overloaded any of the Picture Words in it.

If you have, end your first revised sentence with that Picture Word. (This fits right in with your first rule of simplification: *To make an idea more simple, break it up into a number of short sentences.*)

And then start the next sentence with a repetition of that Picture Word, plus the proper Connectors.

(Once again, this fits right into your second simplification rule: *Use as many Connectors as possible to link up those sentences.*)

So that's our troubleshooting rule. Let's look now at another example, and see how it continues to help us simplify fast and accurately:

"Every day when they came back from school the four older children would play outside in the garden if it was pleasant and indoors when it was raining or too cold."

This example, again, is from a children's book. Again, our first step in simplifying it is to pick out the images in it, and number them. Like this:

"(1) Every day when they came back from school ... (2) the four older children would play ... (3) outside in the garden if it was pleasant ... (4) and indoors when it was raining or too cold."

The big problem here, of course, was where to close off the second image. At first glance it seemed that this image should be: *The four older children would play outside in the garden.*

But this choice leaves the next image, *if it was pleasant,* hanging in mid-air. And, most important of all, it overloads the Picture Word *play.* Because it makes *play* serve in two images: *The four older children would play,* and *(would play) outside in the garden if it was pleasant.*

So, the sheer task of separating our images points out to us immediately the overloaded Picture Word in this sentence (play). And gives us the clue to making it as simple as possible.

Like this:

Simplification 1. Every day when they came back from school is perfectly clear. So we leave it alone, and go on to our next image.

Simplification 2. The second image is: *the four older children would play.* But we now know that *play* is overloaded in the original version. So we end the first revised sentence right here.

And we have:

"Every day when they came back from school, the four older children would play."

Perfectly clear so far. So we go on to:

Simplification 3. This starts with our third image: *outside in the garden if it was pleasant.*

We want, now, to convert this image into a complete sentence. And we want to start it with a repetition of the previously overloaded Picture Word, *play.*

So we simply add the condensing Connector *they,* and get this second revised sentence:

"They would play outside in the garden if it was pleasant."

Simplification 4. And now we go to the fourth image: *and indoors when it was raining or too cold.*

Here we have two choices. First, we can simply make this image into a sentence as it is. Then the complete though-sequence would read:

"Every day when they came back from school, the four older children would play. They would play outside in the garden if it was pleasant. And indoors when it was raining or too cold."

Here, sentence structure expectation serves as the connection between the second and third sentences. It is certainly understandable. But it is not as simple as it could be.

To add greater simplicity to it, we would once again use the same repetition that we used in the second sentence: *They would play.* Thus, we would have the following complete thought sequence:

"Every day when they came back from school the four older children would play. They would play outside in the garden if it was pleasant. And they would play indoors when it was raining or too cold."

And that's all there is to it. A simple procedure that produces simple sentences.

I'll give you several more examples of this procedure in the exercises for this chapter. There, you can put the procedure to work for yourself. And, once you've got the feel of it, you can then go on to use it to correct your own confusing sentences as they come up.

But one extra caution has to be added here. This procedure will work only if the thoughts in the original sentence are in the correct logical order to begin with.

If, however, the original sentence has several images in it, and the order of those images is all jumbled up, then your first step has to be to put them back into correct order.

Only then can you separate the images ... find the overloaded words, and unload them ... shorten the sentences so they contain only one or two images each ... and put in the proper Connectors to tie them all together.

Another example is called for here, to point this out to you. This time, let's leave children's books behind, and turn to one of the most difficult subjects ever conceived by the minds of humans – economics.

This is a sentence from a book on economics, written for the average person. Let me emphasize that it is not a textbook. It is meant for the average person, with a layman's knowledge of the field.

Here it is:

"After the 1929 crash, the business community, President Hoover, and state and local governments failed to distinguish between the money panic caused by the stock market gambling and the strains created by the structural weaknesses in the real basic economy; and most particularly, they failed to comprehend how deeply depressed wages and salaries were in relation to output potential and the inadequacies of consumer credit."

Yes, this is a single sentence, published in a book for the average reader. Its author is a vastly educated man. Yet he has put at least nine different abstract images into this one sentence with only one real road-sign Connector to show his reader how they are related.

And, equally bad, he jumbled up the order of these images so badly that you can't tell which of them is the most important, which causes which, or even what he wants you to think about them.

So, if you had written this sentence, your first task now would be to go over these images, and put them in the right order.

And you would do it something like this:

First, you would identify what the sentence is really talking about. As far as I can tell, it seems to be this:

- That the 1929 crash produced two economic problems.
- That none of the national leaders recognized these problems.
- And, specifically, that they didn't recognize how serious these problems were.

This is the logical order of the thoughts in the original sentence. Once you rephrase it this way, it makes sense. One part follows another. And you are now ready to "flesh out" this logical skeleton with the details themselves.

Here's how one final version would look. Read it through, compare it to the original, and then we'll see why we made the simplifications that we did. (I've italicized the new elements for you.)

"After the 1929 crash, *there were two basic problems facing the country:*

First, the money panic, *which had been caused* by the stock market gambling.

And second, the downturn in production, which had been caused by the structural weaknesses in the real basic economy.

Both were critical. But the business community did not distinguish between *them. Nor did* President Hoover. *Nor did* the state and local governments.

Because of this failure in vision, none of these three power centers comprehended the seriousness of the two main structural weaknesses in the real basic economy. They were:

That wages and salaries *were now too far* depressed *to allow full industrial* output.

And, equally serious, that consumer credit *was no longer* adequate to *finance this full output."*

So one sentence has been simplified into eleven. At least twenty connecting phrases have been added. And the thought-flow has been made far more understandable.

Once again, let's examine exactly what happened here, step by step. Let's see exactly how each simplification was created:

Simplification 1. Our first problem was this. The author did not tell the reader, at the beginning of the original sentence, what the sentence was going to be all about.

Thus, the reader was plunged right into a mass of detail. And had no way of knowing which part of this detail was most important.

So our first step is to give the reader an introduction. To signal in advance the content of this thought-flow, before we actually develop it.

We have done this with our first revised sentence, most of which we created ourselves:

"After the 1929 crash, *there were two basic problems facing the country."*

Here we have used the road-sign phrase *there were.* We have used it to signal the reader in advance about the identity-relationship between the *two basic problems* in the first sentence, and the detailed description of those problems in the second and third sentences.

Simplifications 2 and 3. These problems were, as you remember:

"First, the money panic, *which had been caused by* the stock market gambling."

"And *second,* the downturn in production, *which had been caused by* the structural weaknesses in the real basic economy."

Notice how these two problems are tied in even more closely to the introductory sentence by the use of *numerical order.* Thus, the first sentence says "there were *two* basic problems." And the next sentence says *"First,* the ..." And the next sentence says, *"And second,* the ..."

Notice also how the connecting phrase *which had been*

caused by is repeated in the second and third sentences, to tie them even more closely together.

And notice that we have added *the downturn in production* to the third sentence. This was the real problem caused by the structural weaknesses in the basic economy. But the author did not specifically name it until the end of the original sentence, where it was too late to be understood. So we have added it here, where it should go.

So now we have the first three sentences closely tied together. In them, we have told our reader that there are two main problems. And we have gone on to name them.

Simplification 4. And now we want to leave them behind. And go on to our next core idea – that *"the business community, President Hoover, and state and local governments failed to distinguish between them."*

But we want to make this transition in a perfectly clear way. And the first step in doing this is to signal our reader that we are going to leave the two basic problems.

We do this with the summary sentence: "Both were critical." Here we use the condensing Connector, *both.* And then combine it with *were critical,* to give the reader one last backward look at their seriousness.

Simplification 5. And now we want to move on to our next core idea: The failure of the nation's leaders to respond to the crisis.

We make this transition in the next sentence:

"But the business community did not distinguish between them."

This sentence starts with the road-sign Connector *but.* This tells the reader that our thought is changing direction. And then we shift focus into *the business community did not distinguish between them.*

Once again, this is a new focus. It is concerned, not with the problems themselves, but with the leaders' reactions to them.

The reader's attention is now directed on to this new core idea. But we still tie it in to the first main thought once more by the use of the condensing Connector *them* at the end of this sentence.

Thus, our transition from one core idea to another has first been signaled in advance. Then accomplished. And then tied in both front and back.

Simplifications 6 and 7. Now, in the next two sentences *(Nor did President Hoover. Nor did the state and local governments.)*, we leave the first core idea completely behind us. We are no longer concerned with the problems at all. We are, instead, focusing entirely on one reaction after another.

Here we slice up the sentences even smaller. We slow the pace. We let each reaction stand out bluntly in a separate sentence.

And we connect these three reactions together by two Connectors working at once: By the Connecting Word *nor.* And by repetition in all three sentences of *did.*

Simplification 8. So now our reader has the basic problem, and knows the leaders' reactions to them. Now we want to go on again. We want to bring him into closer focus on the two main reasons for the downturn in production.

This is our third core idea. And we make the transition into it the same way we did before – step by step.

Our first step is to signal the reader that we are going to leave the second core idea. We do this in the first image of sentence 8.

"Because of this failure in vision, none of these three power centers comprehended the two main structural weaknesses on the real basic economy."

The italicized part of this sentence summarizes our second core idea. It waves it goodbye.

It then leads directly into *the two main structural weaknesses in the real basic economy.* This is the reader's introduction to the next core idea. It tells her that we are now going to take a closer look at these two main structural weaknesses.

Simplification 9. This reinforces our introductory-signal with the next connecting sentence: *They were:*

Simplifications 10 and 11. And then we have, in the last two sentences, the two reasons why full industrial output was now impossible.

"That wages and salaries were now too far depressed to allow full industrial output.

And, equally serious, that consumer credit was no longer adequate to finance this full output."

These sentences are connected to the preceding flow of thought by the Connectors *That* and *And that*. They are connected to each other by the connecting phrase in the last sentence *equally serious*.

And they both feature, once again, an expansion of the author's thought. So that the reader has as much detail as she needs, when she needs it, to thoroughly understand what the author is saying.

This, then, is the simplification of this completely confusing piece of writing. I hope it helps prove one thing to you:

It is not subject matter that causes your reader difficulty. It is not your images or your Picture Words, no matter how abstract.

Difficulty is caused by misuse. It is caused by these four kinds of misuse:

First and foremost, *by the misuse of Connectors*. By not putting into your sentences the right Connectors – and the right number of Connectors.

Secondly, *by overloading*. By asking your Picture Words to do too many jobs at once. And thus by making your sentences too long, with too few Picture Words and supporting Connecting Words in them.

Thirdly, *by illogical order*. By not prearranging your thoughts in step-by-step order.

And finally, *by leaving out necessary facts*. By not giving your reader everything he has to know to understand you immediately.

These are the causes of difficulty. All of them can be corrected. Therefore, difficulty can be eliminated – it can be replaced by simplicity – when you do the following:

Put in the right Connectors. And the right number of Connectors to show every relationship between your Picture Words.

Never let a Picture Word do more than one job at a time.

Shorten your sentences. Repeat overloaded Picture Words. Put in all the necessary details. And get them in the right order.

These, then, are the fundamental working rules of simplification. Using them, you need never write a difficult or confusing sentence again.

And now let's elaborate them a bit. And examine some *simplification structures* that put them to work. And that help you in your own communication.

These *simplification structures* are really *patterns of Connectors* that have evolved out of our language as it has been used over the centuries.

They are ready-made ways to arrange your images, so that your reader can most easily absorb them.

Here are some of the best of them:

1.   *Normal Sentence Structure.*

This is simply the conventional sentence form – the form in which we all prefer to receive our information. It consists of an actor ... then an action or identification ... and then usually the person or thing acted upon or made identical. Its two main forms are:

I hit Harry. And

He is a bastard.

The more closely you follow this normal sentence structure, the easier it is for your reader to absorb your thought-flow. But, as we have just seen, there are two ways to violate it that automatically cause difficulty for your reader.

First, you can *overload* it. Squeeze too many details into it.

And second, you can *condense* it. Omit necessary details from it.

We have seen how to correct both these violations. You will have much more practice in doing this in the exercises that follow.

However, the point I wish to make here is this: *Normal sentence structure is the easiest way for your reader to absorb your thoughts.* Therefore, most of your sentences in any discourse should be packaged in this form.

2. *Expansion of Normal Sentence Structure.*

We first encountered this simplification structure in Chapter 4. As you remember, it starts with the normal sentence structure. Then splits off the last phrase of that sentence ... and repeats its structure in as many continuing sentences as are needed to make a series of points completely clear.

For example:

Now it makes sense. *Perfect sense.*

Or:

You can *see it. Smell it. Taste it. Touch it. Draw it. Show it on movie film.*

You can make this image-expansion with any part of the sentence you wish. It can be a single Picture Word at the end of the sentence. Or a connecting phrase. Or the entire sentence outside of the first word.

In any case, you take the structure you have set up in your first sentence, and carry it over into a series of smaller, reinforcing, and expanding follow-up sentences.

These follow-up sentences give you several possible advantages to choose from:

First, they allow you to vary the length of your sentences. To break up a monotonous sentence flow. To build pace and variety into the type of sentences you feed your reader. (We'll see several examples of this in the next chapter.)

Second, they allow you to concentrate your reader's attention on an important point. Short sentences give emphasis to individual details. Your reader stops. Gives her complete attention to each detail. Digests it thoroughly before she goes on to the next.

Third, they allow you to "walk your reader around" that important point. To examine it from every angle. To give as many reinforcing examples as you wish. *("... see it. Smell it. Taste it. Touch it. Draw it. Show it on movie film.")*

And fourth, they lead directly into the next simplification structure. Which is:

3.   *Repetition of Key Phrases.*

This is simply the carrying over of a key image or phrase from one sentence to a second, and then perhaps to a third, fourth, and so on. But each time the phrase is repeated, it is also expanded. So that each time the reader gains more information about it, at the same time that it is kept constantly in front of him.

For example, from Chapter 1:

"There are Picture Words that show us things. Ship. World. Betty ...

There are Picture Words that show us actions. Hit. Sleep. Run ...

There are Picture Words that show us colors. Red. Green. Orange ...

There are Picture Words that show us size. Tall. Fat. Long ...

There are Picture Words that show us details of other pictures. Torn. Embroidered ...

There are Picture Words that show us feelings. Joy. Hate. Love ..."

And so on. Here, almost the complete sentence is repeated. This is done so the reader will understand that all the classifications, and examples, are all simply divisions of the core idea, *Picture-Words.*

But you can also use repetition to detail a process. To show its development. To expand it step by step till the reader sees it from beginning to end. Like this:

Now, once again, what we do with these Picture Words and Connecting Words is this: *We put them together.*

We put them together to tell other people our thoughts.

We put them together into those larger units of thought that we call sentences."

Here, the process of *putting words together* is run through from beginning to end for the reader. It starts with the two types of words themselves. Then it shows how they are put together into thoughts. Then it shows how these thoughts are divided up into logical units called sentences.

But this is a complicated process. In following it through

to the end, the reader might lose the original thought. We carry that original thought along with us through every step in the process – through repetition – so she can't possibly get lost.

One last point: As we have already seen, repetition is a vital tool in eliminating overloaded sentences, and overloaded images.

This point deserves an additional example here. Let's say you are writing a report. In it, you have the following sentence:

"We must be able to detect, in advance, the Turning Point, where a beneficial process becomes suddenly and invisibly harmful."

You can see at once that this sentence is overloaded. Why? Because it contains both a rule *(We must be able to detect, in advance, the Turning Point),* and a definition *(where a beneficial process becomes suddenly and invisibly harmful).*

And you also know exactly where the overloading occurs. With the Picture Word *Turning Point.*

So you decide to stop the sentence there after *Turning Point.* And use repetition as your simplification device. Like this:

"We must be able to detect, in advance, the Turning Point. *The point* where a beneficial process becomes suddenly and invisibly harmful."

4.   *Dependent Sentence Structure.*

These are sentences that signal the reader, with their first word, that they are going to have at least two main parts. And that the first of these parts will be dependent for its full meaning on the second.

In other words – to review again the material we first touched on in Chapter 3 – dependent sentences have this sort of structure:

"If you touch me, I'll scream."

"When you go out, close the door."

"After the party, we had a drink together."

"Unless I'm paid by tomorrow, I'll sue."

The reader is signaled that he is encountering such a dependent sentence by its first word. Some of these first-word signals are: *If ... When ... Unless ... Before ... After ...* and so on.

Such dependent sentences have existed in our language since it was born. They are therefore automatic, natural language devices that show two main types of relationships:

Time *(When ... After ... Before ... etc.).*

Cause and Effect *(If ... Unless ... Because ... etc.).*

They are therefore additional tools for you to use in simplifying your thoughts for your reader. But there are certain rules for employing them most effectively. They are:

First, keep them simple. Don't overload them so much with images that one blocks another.

Here's an example of such overloading:

"If you go down the street and turn the corner and wait fifteen minutes, and still don't get the go-ahead signal, then come back here and ring the bell three times and wait for me to come downstairs and tell you what to do next."

This is pretty simple language – very visual. But it's still almost impossible to understand, or to remember, because there are no pauses in it. The listener can't stop between images, set the first step in her mind, and then go on to the next.

Here's how it should be rewritten:

"Go down the street. Turn the corner. Wait fifteen minutes. If you still don't get the go-ahead signal, then come back here. Ring the bell three times. And wait for me to come downstairs and tell you what to do next."

Which leads us to the second rule for handling these two-part sentences effectively. It is based on the fact that any one of these signal-words (for example, *If)* sets up a question in your reader's mind.

That question is this: What will the second part of the sentence be? (If I do this, what will you do?) Therefore, your reader can't make sense of the first part of your sentence till she knows the second part.

Therefore, she rushes through the first part to discover the second. And therefore, *you should make that first part as short as possible, so the whole sentence becomes as simple as possible.*

You have seen how we did this in the example above. We removed all the detail we could from the first part of the sentence – the *If* part of the sentence. In this way, we reduced this first, introductory part to as short and as simple an image as possible.

Thus, by so doing, we got the reader through that part of the sentence as fast as possible. And therefore got him into the second part, the payoff part of the sentence, soon enough so he wouldn't forget the first.

So our two rules so far are:

Don't let one dependent image block another. And

Keep the first part as short as possible.

Now there's one last rule:

Dependent sentences are fairly self-contained. They concentrate on relationships within the sentence itself. And therefore are not too concerned with relationships with the sentences before and after them.

So you must make sure that they have an extra Connector within them, to tie them in to your overall sentence flow.

Here's how we did this in the example above:

"Go down the street. Turn the corner. Wait fifteen minutes. If you *still* don't get the go-ahead signal, then come back here..."

The Connector, *still,* ties the two-part sentence into the rest of your thought flow. Just as every sentence you write must be tied into that flow.

These, then, are our sentence-structure simplifications: *The normal sentence structure. The expanded sentence structure. The repetition of key words in the expanded sentence structure. And the dependent sentence structure.*

Each one of them can be used to make your thoughts more readily available to your reader. They are built-in simplification structures that your reader is used to, expects, and will understand immediately.

Now let us look at a few others, that depend on different, but equally accepted, structures of thought and communication:

5.   *Number Order.*

This is simply the use of numbers to tell your reader: First, the order of a series of related thoughts. And second, the fact that they all go together.

It uses as its ready-made Connectors the numerals *(1 ... 2 ... 3 ... 4 ...* etc.), or the words that represent these numerals *(First ... Second ... Third ...* etc.).

This book is filled with examples of this device. There is no need to give another here.

6.   *Time Order.*

This is the most commonly used device of both instruction and narration. Here, you simply write your actions in the order in which they happen. You either use numbers to represent this order. Or you use Connectors like *and ... then ... next ... after ...* etc.

All instruction should be organized this way. Take it step by step. Give each step a different paragraph. Number them if necessary. And make sure your reader knows how each step is tied into the next.

This *time order,* in fact, is so powerful that it can be used to organize entire books. Almost all old-fashioned novels used it this way.

It is one of the great simplifying, and therefore organizing, devices. This is because it fits in so well with the way things happen in the real world. And that's what you should always try to make your language do.

Two cautions in using it, however: First, when you start the time sequence, tell your reader in advance that you are going to do so. Give her a *forward-signal,* like this:

"There are six step necessary to build the wing. They take place in this order:"

Then, when you have finished the time sequence, once again tell her that you have done so. Like this:

"Now you have built the wing. You are ready to move on to the landing gear."

And at the same time (as I have done above, with *You are ready to move onto*) connect this sequence to the next sequence.

7.   *Space Order.*

This is another ready-made simplifying device, corresponding to the way things are in reality. But it is far less effective than *time order*, since it has far fewer applications.

It consists simply in describing things in the same order that you would see them. What it does is organize *visual* order for your reader, just as time order organized *temporal* order for him. Like this:

"The raid picked up five men, who were now lined up side by side in the station. The first was a Mexican, about forty, medium height, a scar on his left cheek. Next to him was a Caucasian who might have been sixty, but looked a hundred. And to his right was ..."

And so on. Again, it helps to think of your words as a movie camera for your reader. You are panning from left to right. As long as you keep this sequence, he follows you easily. You are predictable, and therefore simple.

8.   *Forward-Signaling.*

Notice, once again, that in using both time order and space order, we first signaled our reader what was about to come.

This is called *forward-signaling*. It serves two functions. First as a road-sign, to tell him what direction your thought is about to take. And second as a presummary, to tell him how extensive that next unit of thought will be.

Here is how we fulfilled both these functions in our time-order example:

"There are six steps necessary to build the wing. They take place in this order:"

First, we used the forward-signaling Connector *There are*. Then we named the number of steps we were going to give the reader. Then we told her what these steps would accomplish *(build the wing)*.

And then gave her a second forward-signaling Connector, *in this order*. And then we used the forward-signaling punctuation mark the full colon. This showed her, once again, that what was to follow was equal to its summary, which had just been given.

There are, of course, many forward-signaling Connectors, and connecting phrases. Some of them are:

Like this . ..
As follows '"
In this way ...
Let us look at a few others ...
Now let's put them into action ...

Plus any forward-signaling uses of *are*. Such as *There are ... They are ... Some of them are ...*

And remember, your forward-signal is most clear when you do this: Name the number of elements to follow. And tell your reader what it is that all these elements are parts of.

9.   *Summarization.*

This simplification structure consists of doing the same thing at the end of a thought-sequence as you did at its beginning.

Where at the beginning you signaled the reader in advance about the sequence, at the end you summarize the sequence for him.

Here is the example we used in summarizing our time order:

"*Now* you *have built* the *wing*. You are *ready* to *move on* to the *landing gear.*"

First we signaled the reader that the sequence was through by the connecting phrase *Now you have built*. Then we identified again what he had accomplished *(the wing)*.

Then we connected this sequence onto the next sequence with the connection *Now you are ready to move on.* And then we named (forward-signaled) the next sequence – *the landing gear.*

Other summarization Connectors, and connecting phrases, are:

These, then, are ...

So there we have ...

So we now have two types of...

And so on.

So there you have them. Nine ready-made simplification structures, to make your thought easier for your reader.

To these, you add the few Simplification rules you learned at the beginning of this chapter. And you should be able to build into your thought-flow any degree of simplicity you wish.

You should be able to make every sentence in that flow so simple, in fact, that your reader understands it the instant she encounters it.

That means that you have done the work of understanding for her. In advance. So that the connections are built in for her. The relationships are clearly marked out for her. And she never has to stop and go back to find them out for herself.

This is simplification. It is probably the most valuable characteristic you can build into your communication. But it is not the only one. There are other characteristics of good communication, of good grammar-in-action, that you should strive for.

And we will now see how to accomplish them, one by one.

Exercises and Applications
for Chapter 6

In this chapter, you learned how to write a simple sentence. Now you will prove that you can do it.

You also learned how to simplify sentences that somehow came out too complicated. Now you will prove that you can do this too.

In these exercises, fill in the blanks or circle the correct choices.

Let us first review the rules for writing a simple sentence. As you remember, there are, essentially, just two of them.

The first of them is this:

1.   To make an idea more simple, break it up into a number of *(short/long)* sentences.

2.   In other words, the _____ your sentence, the simpler it is.

3.   Simple sentences are _____ sentences.

4.   Therefore, to express a complicated idea to someone else, your first step in making it simple is to break it up into a number of _____ sentences.

5.   Even dependent sentences (for example, *"If you touch me, I'll scream."*) should be kept as *(short/long)* as possible.

6.   So that's the first rule to help you write a simple sentence.

The second rule is this:

To relate the images within that sentence, use as many *(Connectors/details)* as necessary to make sure that your reader understands those relations.

7.   And, to link up one sentence to another, use as many _____ as you need to make sure that your reader understands the way these two sentences relate.

8.   You relate Picture Words, and sentences, and ideas by using _____.

9.   Your reader can't tell how the parts of a sentence go together if you don't give him the right _____.

10.   And your reader can't tell how two adjoining sentences go together if you don't give her the right _____.

11.   So you make sentences simple by first making them _____, and then by putting in the right _____.

12.   Now, when you use a number of sentences together, you add another rule. That rule has to do with the order in which you place these sentences.

You want to place your sentences in *(logical/random)* order.

13.   You want these sentences to start at the beginning, and end at the end. So that if you had to number these sentences, you could *(logically/arbitrarily)* number them 1 ... 2 ... 3 ... 4 ... and so on, right to the end.

14.   Let's say, for example, that you are telling someone how to to do something. You are trying to show him how to do it step by step. You would naturally want these steps to occur in _____ order.

15.   This means that you would want to be able to number these steps, and have your reader agree with that numbering. Because the process of numbering is one way of checking whether or not your thoughts are in _____ order.

16.   So we now have three rules for simplicity. Keep your sentences _____. Use all the _____ you need to tell your reader the relationship between them. And place those sentences in _____ order.

That's our theory. Now let's put it to work.

We can't do it, of course, by asking you to write a simple sentence. Because you never write just one sentence at a time.

So we're going to ask you to write a stream of sentences, a short discourse. Like everyone else, you're an expert at something. You know how to do something better than anyone else.

It may be baking a cake. Or building a model plane. Or fixing a broken window. Or a hundred other things.

In any case, you know how to do it. You know how to do

it well. And I want you to show someone else how to do it here.

Here's how you're going to do this: You're going to break that job down into steps. You're going to write a separate sentence for each step. And you're going to relate each sentence to the next with the proper Connectors.

You don't have to write the full set of instructions here. That would take too long. So let's just take the first five steps.

Remember, break the job down into such simple steps that each one of them can be stated in a single sentence. It doesn't matter how many steps you use. What does matter is that each step be simple enough to be understood the moment your reader sees it.

17. So now you're ready. Let's start with a forward-signaling sentence to tell the reader what all these steps are going to accomplish for her. And then let's go into the steps themselves.

Write your forward-signaling sentence here. Start it with "Here's how you ..."

_____

_____

18. Now write your first-step sentence here. Either you should number it, or start it with the Connector *First:*

_____

_____

19. Write your second-step sentence here:

_____

_____

20. Write your third-step sentence here:

_____

_____

21. Write your fourth-step sentence here:

_____

_____

22.   And write your fifth-step sentence here:

_____

_____

Now check them. Does each sentence contain only one step? Is that step clear? Does it have enough detail for the reader to understand it immediately?

(If it doesn't have enough detail, then perhaps that step is too big. Perhaps it's really two steps that you've tried to crowd into one. Perhaps, therefore, you should split it up into two, more detailed steps.)

23.   Is each sentence tied into the next sentence with the proper Connectors? Write these Connectors – all of them – here:

Forward-signaling sentence: _____

First-step sentence: _____

Second-step sentence: _____

Third-step sentence: _____

Fourth-step sentence: _____

Fifth-step sentence: _____

Are the steps in logical order? Could you change the order of the steps in any way, to make them clearer?

If everything checks out, fine. You're writing simply and completely. You're transmitting a stream of images to your reader in a way that he can understand them immediately.

Now let's go on to another assignment. This time, we'll use a format that has less built-in structure than a series of how to-do-it steps. So you'll have to add a little more of the logical order yourself.

This time, let's tell someone a story. An incident. Something that happened to you recently, and that you want her to see as clearly as you did then.

Here, of course, the type of order we're going to use is time order. You're going to be told how to place your sentences by the time sequence in which they occurred.

Your introductory sentence here will probably start with a word that identifies the time or place in which the incident occurred. And then the other sentences will follow on an action-by-action basis.

24.   So, right now, write a stream of six sentences, telling your reader something that happened to you in all the detail she needs to see it vividly:

_____

_____

_____

_____

_____

_____

25.   Now let's check again. Start at the beginning, and ask yourself:

Can the reader see each image the moment he reads it? Do some images block others? (If they do, put them in their own sentences.)

Is there enough detail in each sentence? (If not, add it. And if the addition overloads the sentence, break it up into two sentences.)

26.   Does each sentence have the right internal Connectors? Does it have the right between-sentence Connectors? List them here:

First sentence: _____

Second sentence: _____

Third sentence: _____

Fourth sentence: _____

Fifth sentence: _____

Sixth sentence: _____

Does each sentence occur in the proper time sequence? Does one sentence logically develop out of the sentence in front of it? Could you number each sentence, and have your reader agree with your numbering?

If all these questions check out, fine. If, however, you've overloaded or overcomplicated any sentence, simplify it according to the rules we'll review below.

We could go on, of course, with these sentence-stream exercises. We could do explanation streams, and reason-why streams, and persuasion streams, and documentation streams, and all the rest.

But we'll get good practice in these in Chapter 10. And I think we've proven, in these two examples, that you can now string sentences together simply enough to be understood at first glance.

So, right now, let's move on, and prove our second point: That you also have the tools at your command, right now, to simplify overloaded sentences when you encounter them.

To simplify an overloaded sentence, or a stream of overloaded sentences, you use the same three rules we listed above, plus one more.

You remember these three rules, of course. They are:

27.   Break up overloaded and overlong sentences, to keep them _____.

28.   Put in all the _____ they need to make the relations between them perfectly clear.

29.   And make sure that they're placed in _____ order.

30.   These three basic rules have already been reviewed.

Now we add our fourth rule:

Never let a Picture Word be part of more than *(one/two)* image(s) at one time.

31.   If you have used a Picture Word as part of two images, *(stop/continue)* the sentence immediately after it.

32.   Then *(eliminate/repeat)* that same Picture Word as a part of the next sentence.

33.   And put in the right _____ to make sure that the new sentence relates correctly to the one you just stopped short.

34.   So you never let a Picture Word serve as part of more than _____ image(s).

35.   When you find an overloaded Picture Word, you automatically _____ the sentence right there.

36. Then you _____ that Picture Word at the beginning of the next sentence.
37. So those are our four rules. Now let's put them to work.

Let's start with a simple descriptive sentence, like this:

"After a few minutes they brought out of the cage a pinkish bird standing on one leg just like the ones they had seen at the zoo."

The overloaded Picture Word in this sentence is b _____. (I've given you the first letter as a hint.)
38. All right. So we now know that *bird* is overloaded. So what do we do now? We _____ the sentence right after it.
39. Write the new, shortened sentence here:

_____

_____

40. Now start your second sentence by repeating that overloaded word. Like this:

"The bird w _____ standing on ..."
41. Now write the complete second sentence here:

_____

_____

42. And now write the two complete sentences here:

_____

_____

Are these two new sentences easier to understand than the old one? I think you'll agree that the answer is yes.
43. And I think you'll agree that you now have the key to simplifying overloaded sentences like this one. But let's try it again, with this example:

"In the book it says that the delta of Egypt is made of rich, good land that can have four crops in one year while in our country we usually have only one."

The overloaded Picture Word in this sentence is

l_____.

44.   So, if *land* is overloaded, we stop the sentence there.
Write the shortened sentence here:

_____

_____

45.   Now start the next sentence by repeating a variation of
that overloaded Picture Word. As one example, you might
start it by saying:
   "The _____ can have ..."
   Or, you might start it by saying:
   "That Egyptian _____ can have ..."
46.   Write the complete second sentence here. (But I would
suggest that it would read better if you put a comma after
year.)

_____

_____

47.   Now write the complete two sentences here:

_____

_____

   Again, it's simple to make your sentences simple! Your
first step is just to look for an overloaded Picture Word.
   But not all overcomplicated sentences overload their
Picture Words. Some just go on too long. For example:
   "The girls began laughing, pleased to have caused the
boys to be afraid of having lost them on their walk, but
slowly they thought that it would be more fun to be all
together and try to collect leaves, or stones, or any other
of the things they met on the way rather than to lose each
other."
   Here, again, is a real monster. To simplify this one, therefore, we have to use a more deliberate procedure. Like this:
48.   First, we number the images. I believe that there are
at least five of them. You may see more, or fewer. Why not
rewrite the sentence now, and number the images at the

end of each one of them:

_____

_____

_____

_____

_____

_____

_____

Now, here's my version, to compare with your own:

"The girls began laughing, pleased to have caused the boys to be afraid of having lost them on their walk, but slowly they thought that it would be more fun to be all together and try to collect leaves, or stones, or any of the other things they met on the way rather than to lose each other."

Your version may differ from mine, of course. There is no one right way to rewrite this sentence. There are, in fact, probably several. But we can both agree that we can do better than the original author.

So, where your points coincide with mine, follow my version. Where they don't, follow your own. But be sure that your new sentences read simply to you when you go over them again.

So, following my version for a moment, we see that Image 1 makes a pretty good sentence, all by itself. So we end our first new sentence there. Write that sentence here:

_____

_____

49. Now, do you think that Image 2 would also make a good sentence by itself, if you gave it a new beginning?

_____

_____

50. If your answer is yes (as mine would be), how would you start that second sentence? Would you use a condensing Connector to carry the image of *the girls* along in that second sentence?

If so, what condensing Connector would you use? T _____.

51. Then you'd need one more word, after *They*, to connect *They* with the rest of the original image. This word should be the identity Connector w _____.

52. So now write your revised second sentence here:

_____

_____

53. These are your first two new sentences. You made them up out of the first two original images. Now go on to Image 3.

Image 3 can also be made into a complete sentence, just as it is. Write this sentence here:

_____

_____

This is fine as it stands. But if we leave it alone this way, we do run into trouble with Images 4 and 5. Why? Because they're out of logical order.

54. I believe that Images 4 and 5 are reversed. In other words, that Image 5 should come before 4, rather than after it.

Try it now. Write the images in a new order here. Write them in order: 3-5-4:

_____

_____

Doesn't this read better? Images 3 and 5 just seem to go together. They make good sense that way. Much better sense than they made the old way.

So let's use this new order. Once we do, our next decision is where to stop our third revised sentence.

We've already experimented with it like this:

"But slowly they thought that it would be more fun to be all together..."

Then we tacked on to the end of it the remaining two images:

"... rather than to lose each other and try to collect leaves or stones, or any of the other things they met on the way."

Now, how do we combine all these images into simple sentences? I think we can agree that 5 and 4 don't go together at all. In fact, they're downright confusing if we leave them together.

55.   But what about 3 and 5 in a single sentence? Do you think that they would make a good sentence together? *(Yes/No)*.

56.   If your answer is yes, write that sentence here. Use the proper punctuation mark between the two images, of course.

_____

_____

So now we have the following three revised sentences:

"The girls began laughing. They were pleased to have caused the boys to be afraid of having lost them on their walk. But slowly they thought that it would be more fun to be all together, rather than to lose each other."

And we have only the last image, *and try to collect leaves, or stones, or any of the other things they met on the way,* to deal with.

This image cannot be converted into a complete sentence without being changed. Why? Because it lacks the proper Connectors to tie it in with the other sentences.

57.   What kind of Connectors, therefore, shall we use? Here's what I would suggest:

First of all, a cause-and-effect Connector. This Connector should answer the question: Why did the girls want to be with the boys again?

The answer, of course, is because then they could all try

to collect objects they met along the way.

This is the logical connection between this last sentence and the ones that came before it. It can be expressed by either one of two Connectors: b_____, or t_____. Or it can be expressed by both of them, as it was in the sentence above.

58. So this gives us our cause-and-effect tie-in to the sentence that came before. Now we have to choose a condensing Connector to carry forward the image of the boys and the girls. That condensing Connector is t _____.

59. So now you have the complete last sentence, minus only one word. Fill in that word now:

"Because then they c _____ try to collect leaves, or stones, or any of the other things they met on the way."

So that is your complete simplification. It looked hard at first. But it was actually quite simple, once you broke it down step by step.

I feel that I should call your attention, once again, to a technique you used in this last simplification. That is the technique of detecting when images are out of logical order.

We did this, as you remember, on Images 3, 4, and 5. We felt that they were out of order, that they were reversed.

What made you feel this way? The fact that they didn't make sense when we first read them. That *and try to collect leaves, or stones, or any of the other things they met on the way* blocked the completion of *it would be more fun to be all together, rather than lose each other.*

The original order of the sentences was wrong; therefore, the cause-and-effect relationship in those sentences was wrong. The boys and the girls had to join together again before they could all begin to collect what they found. Only when they got together could they collect together.

The order of your sentences must make sense. First events must come first. Second events must come second. The world these sentences create must work in exactly the same order as the world they represent.

If that written world doesn't work in the same sequence

as the physical world around it, change its sequence. Change it at the very place where it departs from the real world. This is your key to simplifying your thought flow.

So, if images in your sentences seem jumbled up when you reread them, try shifting them around to see if they come out better.

I think we should look at one more example of this kind of problem, because you do encounter it so many times. And because it does look so bewildering at first glance.

Here is a real monster:

"Some plum trees full of fruit that would be ripe very soon, and some apple trees, with apples too small to be eaten, were the trees he knew."

This kind of reversal is fairly classic. It happens all the time. And it's easy to correct.

You know at first glance that the logical order here is way out of line. You know this because of your familiarity with normal sentence structure.

In normal sentence structure, the first thing you see is the actor of the sentence. Then the action. And then the things acted upon.

Here, however, the sequence is completely reversed. So you have to set it right.

60. You do this by first identifying the actor in the sentence. The actor here is _____.

61. Then you pick out the action. The action here is

_____.

62. So the first two words of your revised sentence are:

_____.

From this point on, you have a number of choices. Let's number the images in the original sentence, and explore them.

63. I believe that there are three main images in the original sentence. Write the original sentence here, and number the images:

_____

_____

64.   Here is my version:

"Some plum trees full of fruit that would be ripe very soon, and some apples trees, with apples too small to be eaten, were the trees he knew."

We started our revised sentence flow, of course, with Image 3. Thus, we started with *He knew, ...* Now we have to add some Connector between these words and *trees*.

I would suggest this first sentence:

"He knew some of the trees."

Then I would use repetition to connect Image 1 to this first revised sentence. What two words would you repeat, to start your second revised sentence? _____

65.   Now write your complete second sentence:

_____

_____

Where did you stop that second sentence? At the end of the original Image 1? Or at the end of Image 2?

Either is correct. Both are simple enough to be understood the moment they are first read.

So here are the two alternate complete thought-flows – in case you'd like to check them:

"He knew some of the trees. He knew some plum trees full of fruit that would be ripe very soon, and some apple trees, with apples too small to be eaten." Or:

"He knew some of the trees. He knew some plum trees full of fruit that would be ripe very soon. And he knew some apple trees, with apples too small to be eaten."

The second version is more careful than the first. It uses smaller sentences. It repeats *he knew* one more time. It therefore can be read, for example, by younger readers more easily than the first version.

But, since the images here are so very simple, I believe that version one will also do very well. It seems to be a matter of style – the style you wish to choose.

We will touch more deeply on this matter of style in the

next chapter. But, for now, the important thing is that you know how to take a jumbled monster like the first sentence, and convert it into the kind of simplicity that both final versions represent.

So you have proved your ability to simplify. And you have learned how to write simple sentences in the first place, so you don't have to use that ability except on rare occasions.

We could do many more of these simplification exercises, of course. But the same rules apply in all of them. And you use them in the same way.

And, most important, the best practice is always your own writing. This is where the payoff comes. And this is where you should apply these rules, over and over again, until they become automatic.

The goal, as I've said before, is this: To plan two or three sentences ahead, before you speak them or put them down on paper. To simplify them in your head before you write them. So you get them right in the first place. And revision is therefore unnecessary.

After a while, you'll be able to "feel" an overloaded sentence forming in your mind. Just as a tennis player "feels" when she's out of position for the next shot.

And you'll be able to stop that sentence short, and pull out that overload, and regain your flow of simplicity. Just as a top tennis player flows back into correct position before her opponent can make the next shot.

And, once you get the hang of it, you'll find that writing simple sentences is far easier than writing complicated ones. Why? For two reasons:

First, because you're forced to make your thoughts sharp. Long, sloppy, overloaded thoughts just won't work when you want to write simply. To simplify them, you have to sharpen them. And thus you, yourself, see more clearly what you really want to say.

And second, because you have to keep your thoughts in logical order. They just can't wander all over the place any more. So you use the logical structures that our language has evolved over the centuries.

And you use them deliberately, not only as ready-made patterns to help you arrange your own thoughts, but also as powerful tools of working thought through to the proper conclusions.

We have already examined some of these logical structures in this chapter. Here, we called them *simplification structures.*

You have had a good deal of practice in using these simplification structures in the exercises we have just done. You will have more practice in using them in the next chapter.

Then, in Chapter 10, we will examine even more logical structures. These will be of wider application, powerful enough to organize entire chapters of a book, or the entire book itself.

So, our goal is this: When you have finished learning these mental tools, you should be able to write your thoughts simply from beginning to end. And you should also be able to carry them to their logical conclusions, so that your reader understands everything you want to say.

Chapter 7

How to Avoid Monotony — So that Your Reader Enjoys Your Sentences at the Same Time that He or She Learns From Them

T HIS CHAPTER IS something of a footnote to the previous one. We now know how important simplicity is. But when you build simplicity, you can also run into an opposing danger – monotony.

The reason for this is quite logical. Simplicity emerges, as we have seen in the last chapter, from making sentences short, making Connectors apparent, and from using the most familiar sentence structures as often as possible.

Simplicity therefore has a tendency to result in a series of short, choppy sentences – all of which have the same "actor ... action ... object-acted-upon" structure.

If this type of sentence structure is continued too long, it intrudes upon the reader's attention. And she finds herself seeing the *sentences,* rather than their *content.* And this becomes not only distracting, but irritating.

Thus, simplicity must be balanced. It must be balanced with two other, less important, communication goals.

The first of these is *variety.* The second is *emphasis.*

Let us now examine how you use each of them to break up

your simplicity when you feel that's necessary, and keep it from obtruding into your reader's consciousness.

The first way to do this is through *variety*. It is quite a simple process, which consists of *purposely changing the length and structure of your sentences when you find them becoming boring.*

Remember, you now have many different types of sentence structures to work with. You have, in fact, an inventory of sentence structures. Some of them are:

1.   The normal sentence, with its Connector in the middle. For example: *"He is, in fact, my son."*

2.   The normal sentence, with its Connector at its beginning. For example: *"In fact, he is my son."*

3.   The dependent sentence, with its Connector in the middle. For example: *"If there is any trouble, then call me."*

4.   The dependent sentence, with its Connector at its beginning. For example: *"Then, if there is any trouble, call me."*

5.   The expanded sentence, with its expansion based on the last word of the previous sentence.

For example: *"She must have had at least one lover before you. Or before Harry. Or Sam. Or Joe."*

As you can immediately see, you can carry this out through one expansion. Or two. Or three. Or more. Thus, any expanded sentence structure gives you a whole series of possible variations.

6.   The expanded sentence, with its expansion based on a middle word, or phrase, of the previous sentence.

For example: *"She must have had at least one lover before you. Or two. Or three. Or four."*

7.   The expanded sentence, based on normal sentence-structure expectation.

For example: *"This is important. For two reasons."*

8.   The expanded sentence, based partially or totally on repetition.

For example: *"You can see it. Feel it. Taste it. Smell it."*

9.   The forward-signaling sentence.

For example: *"For example:"*

10. The single-word sentence, which gains its meaning

from the sentence preceding it.

For example: *"How many people paid $100 a ticket? None."* And so on. These are only the first ten. And they are only variations in the *sentence structure* itself.

But there are other variations you can also use. You can take the same sentence structure – let's say the normal sentence structure – and vary it according to the number of words you use in it, and according to the number of images.

Let's see how you do this:

First, you can vary it as to number of words. It can, of course, be as short as two words *(I itch)*. Or – still retaining its simplicity – it can go up to a dozen or more words: *I have a terrible itch right here beneath my left shoulder blade.*

Or, you can take any word in that normal sentence, and replace it with a multi - word image.

For example:

You can use an image as the actor: *"The most beautiful woman I have ever seen* is going to become my wife tomorrow."

Or you can use an image (or even more than one image) as the action: "So we *walked and talked and held each other and fell desperately in love."*

Or you can use an image as the thing acted upon: "I saw *birds rising toward the sun with wings black as Satan."*

Or you can use an image as a result of the action: "I hit him in the nose so hard *that it didn't stop bleeding for an hour."*

And so on. It is all a question of how much detail you can add to each sentence, and still have your reader understand each image as she encounters it. For you still must keep each new varied sentence ... understandable, as well as varied.

So you have to establish a balance. If your words are simple, and your images are visual, then your sentences can be longer.

If, however, your words are difficult, and your images are abstract, then your sentences must be shorter.

The same rule holds true for your relationships. If these relationships are apparent – as they are for a story based on ordinary time-sequences – then your sentences can be longer.

If, however, these relationships are not apparent, or are unfamiliar to your reader, then you must give each of them its own sentence.

Here, then, is the general rule:

The simpler the thought, the longer the sentence that can still be instantly understood.

But the moment your reader has to stop in the middle of your sentence, and figure out for himself your meaning, then that sentence is too long.

At that point, stop the sentence. Simplify it until it becomes immediately understandable again.

As you can see, then, simplicity forms the outer limit to your variations. You never build a sentence with so many words in it that it cannot be immediately understood.

But, within this one limit, you have hundreds of variations. In normal sentence structure alone, there are dozens of ways that you can vary the word content, and still keep it simple.

Keeping this limit in mind, let's look at another way you can vary your normal sentence structure. This is by taking two thoughts, which could be written as separate sentences, and combining them into a single sentence with the proper Connector.

For example: *"I have known him for fifteen years. He is a fine man."*

This could be written: *"I have known him for fifteen years and he is a fine man."*

Here, the key is obviously the simplicity of each of the two separate sentences. If they are both instantly understandable, *and if the relationship between them is also instantly understandable,* then you can combine them.

What is an instantly understandable relationship? One that can be expressed by the simplest Connectors, such as *and,* and *but,* and *and* then.

So, on occasion, to vary your sentence flow, you can combine two simple sentences into one simple sentence. But the test is always simplicity. And you apply the test in this way:

After you have written your sentences, leave them for a

day. And then come back to them cold the next day. If you can
understand each of them instantly, fine. If you can't, simplify.

Simplicity is always more vital than variety. If you must
choose between the two, choose simplicity.

But you can have both. You can have variety within the
limits of simplicity. You can have variety by interweaving
the hundreds of simple sentence variations that are available to you. You can use different sentence structures. And
you can use different sentence lengths.

And by doing so – by using them all – you need hardly
repeat the same type or length of sentence on a single page.

And still, every one of your sentences will be instantly
understood – which is always the ultimate goal.

Now, let's go on to the second way to avoid monotony.
And this is *emphasis.*

Emphasis is *the process of making certain thoughts stand*
out in your sentence flow.

Not all of your thoughts, of course, are main thoughts.
Some are vital. Others are merely details. You want to
separate the two for your reader.

You do this by emphasis. And, in using emphasis, you
also gain another way to avoid monotony.

Now, how do you create emphasis? Primarily by the use
of three devices we have already discussed:

- *Pointing out.*
- *Repetition.*
- *Shortening your sentences.*

The first emphasis device is *pointing out.* Here, *you tell the*
reader that what you are going to say is important. You point
out its importance to her. You emphasize that importance.

There are, of course, dozens of ways of doing this. I have
used many of them in this book. Some of them are:

- *Italicizing.* You *italicize* those sentences that are especially important. (Or, if you are writing with a pen
  or typewriter, you underline them.) Therefore, they
  stand out.
- *Forward-signaling.* You say bluntly to the reader that

what you are about to say is important. You use such sentences as: *"This is the vital point ... Here is my main theme ... Pay special attention to this point."*

- *Summation.* You tell the reader, again bluntly, that what you have just said is important. Or you point out to him the core-meaning of a series of points you have just finished.

  To do this, you use such summary sentences as: "So we have now seen the three main causes *for the Depression* ... These, then, are the three easiest ways *to reduce production costs"* ... and so on.

This, then, is the first way to produce emphasis: By pointing out to your reader which are your important thoughts.

By doing this, you vary the impact of your sentences. You make her concentrate more heavily on a few of them. And you allow her to skim more lightly over the remainder.

The next way to produce emphasis is *repetition. It is the process of repeating important words, images, and sentences to call them again and again to your reader's attention.*

Here you return, again and again, to an important idea in your thought-flow. By such repeated return, you give it added visibility and significance.

We have already seen several examples of this emphasis by repetition. Here is one more of them:

"I love you today. *I shall love you* tomorrow. *I shall love you* next year. *And I shall love you* throughout eternity."

All of these are simple normal sentences. But, by repetition of a highly charged image, they explode off the page.

Our third way of producing emphasis is simply to *shorten our sentences.* Slowing down the pace of our sentences. Making our images shorter and shorter. With more and more stops in between them.

This is much like a technique used in the movies. Where a single frame is frozen on the screen for a moment or two. And the viewer cannot escape concentrating on it.

Again, we have seen many examples of this shortening technique. But before, they were used for another purpose

– to simplify our sentences.

Now we are using them, not only to simplify, but primarily to emphasize. To slow the reader down, and call his attention to this particular image.

When we inject this kind of emphasis into our sentence-flow, we go beyond the demands of simplicity. We isolate images into so many separate sentences that the reader becomes aware of this isolation. She notices it. And it therefore emphasizes the image it isolates.

As we do in this example:

"If you want to master mathematics, you must learn one thing. To take each problem step by step. Step by step. Step. By. Step."

Unusual. Startling. And therefore, powerful. Emphasis by sentence shortening. Even beyond the demands of simplicity. (Though it can still be understood immediately.)

These, then, are the two devices for avoiding monotony in your sentences: *variation* and *emphasis*.

They both operate within the limits of simplicity – although they operate in different directions:

Variation allows you to "add exotic flavors" to certain sentences. To change both their structure and the number of images they contain.

Emphasis allows you to shorten them, and build repetition into them, until both the repetition and the shortening become apparent, and they stand out.

And when you combine the two devices together, you have an almost infinite number of different sentence-types to choose from.

All of them are simple. All are immediately understood. And yet they protect you from having monotony creep into your communication.

So we have now built simplicity, and variation, into our sentences, without sacrificing enjoyment to do it.

Now let us go on to our next step, and see how we also build clarity into them. And how the same insight that produces this clarity can also lead us to wit, symbolism, and suspense.

**Exercises and Applications
for Chapter 7**

In Chapter 6, you learned how to break overlong sentences down, and transform them into shorter, and more easily understood sentences instead.

In this chapter, you have learned the opposite process. You have learned how to take sentences so repetitious and short that they were annoying the reader, and transform them into longer sentences. These longer sentences add variety to your discourse, but are still easily understood by your reader.

So, in these two chapters, you have been playing the vitally important game of *transformations.* Of expanding and contracting sentence length. Of varying both the size and style of your sentences to express not only your thought, but also your mood and emphasis and feeling.

For different types of sentences do express different moods, and different feelings. For example, a series of short, normal, one-part sentences are direct, clipped, commanding, even harsh.

Like this:

"Go down the stairs. Turn left at the bottom. Walk up the street. Stop at the bakery shop. Wait there fifteen minutes. Karl will contact you then. And he will tell you what to do next."

On the other hand, you may choose to use a series of long, dependent sentences, with many images each. This will give you a much softer, more thoughtful, more hesitant tone.

Like this:

"If you are going to Helen's party tonight, please call me. I had such a charming conversation with you at our last meeting, and the time flew so quickly, that I can hardly wait to renew the experience again. If you need transportation, I shall be glad to arrange it, and will be happy to pick you up at any time you wish."

So these two types of sentence structure give you two different "voices." They allow you to make the tone of your communication loud or soft, hard or sweet, dominant or seductive.

And they do it all within the limits of simplicity. Your reader still understands your thought the moment he encounters it. But now he also picks up a "bonus" message with it – the feeling inside you that accompanies that thought.

This is a side benefit, of course. We did not set out to learn how to convey feelings, but only thoughts.

But language is such a powerful and flexible tool that you cannot study any part of it without learning more than you first anticipated.

So I felt that I must call this side benefit to your attention: When you learn how to shorten sentences to simplify them – and then how to lengthen other sentences to give your discourse variety – what you are doing is learning one of the basic building blocks of *style*.

And *style* means the *ability to convey emotion, and pleasure, over and above the practical goal of conveying thoughts.* So you not only inform your reader, you please her. Once again, it is a side application, but it is a most delightful one.

But we can only touch on style here very briefly, and then we have to return to our main goal – understanding. So our questions now are these:

How long a sentence can you write, and with how many images, and still make it understandable?

And, even more important:

What are the rules for making long sentences as understandable as short ones?

Most of the answers we have already. But let's review them again, in this new context.

As for the world's longest simple sentence, it probably would occur in fiction. Why? For the reason we gave before. That the simpler and more visual the images, and the more apparent the relationships between them, the longer the sentences can be.

Probably the classic example of this fact is the writing of Ernest Hemingway. To illustrate it, I'm going to reproduce here an incredibly long (and magnificent) sentence from "The Short Happy Life of Francis Macomber."

I don't advocate that you write like this. But there is much to be learned from the absolute simplicity and beauty of this man's style.

Here it is:

"The car was going a wild forty-five miles an hour across the open and as Macomber watched, the buffalo got bigger and bigger until he could see the grey, hairless, scabby look of one huge bull and how his neck was part of his shoulders and the shiny black of his horns as he galloped a little behind the others that were strung out in that steady plunging gait; and then, the car swaying as though it had just jumped a road, they drew up close and he could see the plunging hugeness of the bull, and the dust in his sparsely haired hide, the wide boss of horn and his outstretched, wide-nostrilled muzzle, and he was raising his rifle when Wilson shouted, "Not from the car you fool," and he had no fear, only hatred of Wilson, while the brakes clamped on and the car skidded, plowing sideways to an almost-stop and Wilson was out on one side and he on the other, stumbling as his feet hit the still speeding-by of the earth, and then he was shooting at the bull as he moved away, hearing the bullets whunk into him, emptying his rifle at him as he moved steadily away, finally remembering to get his shots forward into the shoulder, and as he fumbled to reload, he saw the bull was down."

Amazing! A single sentence, that happens to be a masterpiece of one man's style.

But our problem is this: How does Hemingway put so very many words in this sentence, and still retain his reader's instant understanding?

The answer is quite simple really: *The entire sentence hinges on time order.* You, the reader, are seeing the sequence exactly as though it were being shown to you on a movie screen.

And not one part of that sequence is out of order. One action directly follows another, as though it were timed by a stopwatch.

In fact, image after image in the sentence reinforces that sense of time passing. For example:

"... as Macomber watched, the buffalo got bigger and bigger ..."

"... and then ... they drew up close and he could see the plunging hugeness of the bull ..."

"... and then he was shooting at the bull as he moved away, hearing the bullets whunk into him ..."

So passing time – film-strip time – is the structure that glues together all these words, without their falling out of order and confusing the reader.

But Hemingway doesn't depend merely on this time structure alone. He reinforces it constantly with time Connectors.

And here's where our analysis of simplicity-in-great-length begins. Now you enter into the picture. Your first question is this:

1.   What is the time Connector Hemingway uses most often to tie his images together in this sentence? a_____

2.   How many times does he use *and* in this sentence? _____

3.   So there are fifteen *and* Connectors in this one sentence. *And,* of course, shows time passing. But there is a more emphatic Connector that also shows time passing, and Hemingway uses it here too. It is a combination of *and* and t _____.

4.   How many times does Hemingway use this *and then* Connector in this sentence? _____

5.   So there are thirteen straight *and's,* and two *and then's.*

But there are also other time Connectors here: *until* ... *as* ... *while* ... *when* ... and *still.*

All in all, how many of these other time Connectors are there in this sentence? _____

So now we have thirteen *ands,* two *and thens,* and nine other time Connectors. Twenty-four Connectors in all, in a single sentence.

So, in summary, Hemingway used two devices to tie together this huge sentence. The first is film-strip time. And the second is a liberal sprinkling of Connectors.

And, in addition, as in all of his writing, there is the utter simplicity of each image as it takes its place in this time-sequence.

And there is the vividness of the images themselves: The power of Hemingway to make us see exactly what he says is happening, and therefore understand it with our eyes.

So, in fiction at least, we know we can write gargantuan sentences, and still keep them simple. This is partially a function of the connecting devices we use, and partially a function of the great power of time-sequence to give order to our images.

But we wish to extend this long-sentence capability to other kinds of communication besides storytelling. We want to be able to lengthen our sentences, when we wish, in report writing, instruction, business correspondence, and all the rest.

6.   How do we do this? What are the techniques that build this capability into our communication? That allow us to make these vital transformations, and still keep them understandable?

Once again, we have already discussed the two negative rules for doing this. As you remember from Chapter 3, they were:

When you start writing sentences with more than one image, you have to keep each image to the point. This means without unnecessary details.

If you want to develop a good deal of detail in any one image, therefore, don't use that image as part of a larger sentence. Split it off, and give it a sentence of its own.

And, secondly, don't let one image block another. As soon as it does, your sentence is confusing.

Read the Hemingway sentence again. Notice that none

of these images blocks another. Instead, there is a straight-line development from beginning to end.

So you must give order to each individual sentence, as well as to your overall sentence flow.

Now, how do you do this? Once again, by planning, and by using Connectors.

And so, now, we move into a new, positive rule. That goes like this:

Certain Connectors can be used as sentence-lengtheners, to give you long sentences that are still instantly understandable.

Such Connectors are the following:

still ...

both ...

not only ...

once ...

and ... (another use for this most versatile Connector)

And many more. These will do to show you the technique. The rest you will pick up as you begin to use them. Once again, it will be valuable for you to draw up your own list.

Now let's see how they're used. Let's start with *both*. And see how we insert it within a sentence to signal our reader, in advance, that we are going to extend that sentence by an image or two.

Here's a typical example:

"I am *both* offended at the bluntness of your offer, and vastly intrigued by the scope of its imagination."

Here, *both* signals your reader, when he is only three words into the sentence, that this sentence will have two images within it.

Thus, your reader expects these two images. She is prepared for them. And she reads the first image with the thought in mind that the second one will follow it immediately, to complete the sentence-idea.

7.   So *both* is your first Connector used as a sentence-lengthener. Now you use it. Write your *both* sentence here:

_____

_____

Not only is used the same way. Here is an example:

"I wish, *not only* to follow you as my leader for the rest of my life, but, if necessary, to give that life in the service of your cause."

Again, a Connector-signal is used here, to tell your reader that the first image in this sentence will express only part of the total thought.

Thus, again, your reader is prepared for the double image to follow. And he is comfortable when he encounters them.

8.   So write your *not only* sentence here:

Once is also used the same way. For example:

"Now, *once* you understand that this girl is desperately in need of love, you can then see quite clearly why she continues to take such abuse from Arthur."

9.   Again, a forward-signal. One that will be of value to you. So put it to work here, in your own *once* sentence:

Notice that all of these forward-signaling Connectors are first cousins of the dependent Connectors we discussed in Chapter 6. They do the same kind of job as *when ... if ... until ...* etc.

The use of them therefore gives you the opportunity to construct understandable two-part sentences. (Or sentences with several parts.)

They do this by signaling your reader in advance that extra images are coming. And they also help arrange these images in logical order, so that they won't block each other when you do combine them.

10.   Now you can also do the same thing with certain Picture Words. These forward-signaling Picture Words are the ones that convey the same meaning of partiality and incompleteness as the Connecting Words we have just examined.

Let's take one example – the Picture Word *partially*. Here's how I have used it as a forward-signal for a multipart sentence just three pages before this one:

"This is *partially* a function of the connecting devices we use, and *partially* a function of the great power of time sequence to give order to our images."

Now write your *partially* sentence here:

_____

_____

So we have a new series of forward-signaling Connectors, which we can use when we want to lengthen our sentences, without sacrificing understandability.

11. But all sentence-lengthening Connectors don't have to be used at the beginning of the sentence. Let's look now at some that can be used in its middle:

The first of them is our old friend, *and*. Here's a new use for it, as a device for adding one extra image to a dependent sentence. Like this:

"If, however, he refuses to be rational, *and* continues to attack you in the press, then I'm afraid that we will have no choice but to sue him."

Notice that the *and* forms the link here between two parallel images. In other words, two images that have similar action words in them: *refuses* and *continues.*

This parallelism is important. You should make sure it's there any time you link two introductory images together in a dependent sentence like this.

Now write your dependent *and* sentence here:

_____

_____

And can also be used later on in a sentence, of course, to link images together in understandable order. We have already seen many examples of this. For instance:

"So we walked *and* talked *and* held each other *and* fell desperately in love."

Or the Hemingway sentence.

And there are other Connectors that do the same length-ening job – again, without sacrificing understandability – in the middle of your sentences. We have already examined *until, as, while, when* and *still* in the Hemingway sentence.

12.   Now let's look at some others. One of the most useful is *to*. It works like this:

"I have accepted this office to bring true democracy back to the American people."

In this sentence, *to* is used two ways. In the phrase *to the American people,* it is used as an ordinary space Connector.

But, earlier in the sentence, *to* is used as the link between *I have accepted this office* and *bring true democracy back to the American people.*

Thus, like many Connectors, it serves us in more than one way. Both as a space Connector, and as a link between two images.

And it relates these two images understandably. The reader has no trouble following the connection between them.

Now you write a *to* sentence that uses it to link two images together:

_____

_____

13.   Another such Connector is *even though*. For example:

"I am not going to walk out on you, *even though* you have given me more pain than any human being I have ever met."

Again, *even though* serves as a logical connection between these two images.

You write your *even though* serves as a logical connection between these two images.

You write your *even though* sentence here:

_____

_____

14.   Another such Connector is *than.* Let's go back to the sample sentence above, and see how it works:

"I am not going to walk out on you, even though you have given me more pain *than* any human being I have ever met."

Write your *than* sentence here:

_____

_____

And so on. The general rule is this:

Any Connector that can link up two images can be used to lengthen your sentences.

The correct way to use this rule is this:

These Connectors can be used to link images together only as long as they do not overload any Picture Words within them.

Or, to phrase it in a different way, as a danger-signal:

If your lengthening process overloads any Picture Word in your sentence, then that sentence is too long, and has to be simplified at that point.

And the rule to determine this is the same one that we've discussed before:

Write your sentences as best you can. Then leave them alone overnight. Then come back to them. If they're not immediately understandable at that time, simplify them.

In other words, the fundamental rule still holds:

Simplicity is more important than length. Or variety. Or style.

When in doubt, simplify.

So there we have it. What it boils down to is this:

Yes, you can write long sentences. And you write them by using the proper Connectors between your images within them.

But these Connectors can also be misused. They are misused when they overload a Picture Word within any sentence.

For example, some very powerful image Connectors are *who, that, which, than,* etc. All can be used to lengthen sentences understandably.

But all of them can also be misused to overload the Picture Words they refer back to.

The opportunity, therefore, is accompanied by a danger. But, fortunately, you can avoid that danger by rechecking those sentences after you have written them.

If the Connectors work – if the Picture Words are not overloaded – keep them.

If they don't work, get rid of them. And build new sentences instead. And begin them with a repetition of the overloaded Picture Words.

So what have we done in these exercises? This:

We've come full circle from where we started. We started with long sentence – but long sentences that were confused.

Then we learned the techniques of making those sentences simple. Techniques that also made those sentences short.

Simplicity breeds shortness. And this shortness, if it's carried too far, may lead to monotony.

So we had to reverse the process. And learn the techniques of building long sentences again.

But this time, using these simplification techniques, we built long sentences that were not confusing. We built long sentences that were simple. Long sentences that could be immediately understood.

And we learned the cut-off point in building such sentences. The point where overloading, and therefore confusion, sets in.

And we accepted this point as a barrier, beyond which we would not go. We accepted the theory that variation can be accomplished within the limits of simplicity. But that it would always be subordinate to such simplicity.

So these exercises have taught us this: That variety, as well as simplicity, is a function of Connectors. And order. And planning.

To strip down, we watch our Connectors. And our order.

To build up, we watch our Connectors. And our order.

And we plan ahead, so we know what we're doing.

So we always have a practical side to our communication

– to transmit our ideas to another person.

And we have an aesthetic side. That of style. Of making her enjoy reading them.

Both result from the same rules. We can have both, without sacrificing either.

Chapter 8

How to Write Clearly —
So Your Reader Doesn't
Think You Mean One Thing,
When You Really Mean Another

A͟T THIS POINT, let me me review for you, once again, the ultimate goal of all grammar, and the means by which we achieve this goal.

The goal is, of course, *communication.* The purpose of grammar is simply *to help you tell other people your ideas.* To transfer your thoughts into their minds.

You do this through words and sentences. Through images and Connectors. Until you have taken an entire flow of thought – a novel, or poem, or business report – and conveyed it intact from your mind to another's.

To do this most easily and effectively, you must be understood every step of the way. So that you never confuse or lose your reader. So that he follows you effortlessly from beginning to end.

Thus, to accomplish this goal of *immediately understanding communication,* you want to build two main characteristics into your writing. They are:

1.   You want it to be *simple,* so that your reader understands every step in your thought, before you take him on to the next.

We have just seen how to do this, whether you write short sentences, or long.

2.   And, at the same time, you want your writing to be *clear*. So that your reader doesn't think that you're saying one thing, when you're really saying another.

Now, up until today, there has been confusion between simplicity and clarity. We really did not have the proper vocabulary to distinguish between them. And therefore we could not learn how to build each one of them into our sentences.

I believe that this confusion is now ended. It has been ended by our prime concept – the difference between Picture Words and Connecting Words. And it has been ended by the new techniques that this basic concept has enabled us to create.

Here is how it works, to make our sentences clear as well as simple:

As you remember, Picture Words carry the images of your thought. And Connecting Words show the relationship between these images.

Without Picture Words, your sentences are empty. And without Connecting Words, they are misunderstood.

The process of building your sentences, therefore, is to first pick out your images. And then pick out the relationships you want to show between them.

When your relationships are immediately understood by your reader (i.e., when they are adequately expressed by the proper Connectors, and when there are not too many of them to be absorbed at once), *then your sentences are simple.*

And *when your images are immediately understood by your reader, then your sentences are clear.*

So you have two conditions a sentence must achieve to be adequately understood. It must be simple. And it must be clear.

Its relationships must be understood. And its images must be understood.

One without the other is not enough. We have already seen that the images in a sentence may be perfectly clear, but that there may be so many of them in that sentence, or the relationships between them may be so poorly expressed, that the reader may have to go over that sentence two or three times to understand it – if she ever does at all.

We have already seen how to correct these unnecessary complications. First, by breaking up the overloaded sentence into series of smaller sentences, each of which can be absorbed instantly.

And, second, by strengthening the Connectors, adding more of them, or making them more visible, so that the relationships are instantly apparent to the reader when she encounters them.

Now, in this chapter, we turn to our second and equally important problem: The sentence in which the relationships are completely understood, but where the images are not clear.

What do we mean by *clear?* We mean this:

A Picture Word, or phrase, is clear when it has only one possible meaning in the sentence in which it is used.

A Picture Word is unclear (ambiguous) when it has more than one meaning in that sentence. And when you did not intend it to have those extra meanings.

Now let's put this definition to work. To do so, we have to look more deeply into the nature of Picture Words.

The big problem with Picture Words is that most of them have more than one meaning. And they shift from one of these meanings to another almost invisibly, before you're even aware of it.

For instance, take the example we used some time ago:

"Ship sails tomorrow."

This is a truly tricky sentence. Because it has two Picture Words in it – *ship* and *sails* – that can each have two different possible meanings in this exact same sentence.

As we have seen, this sentence can either mean:

"Ship the sails tomorrow."

Or:

"The ship sails tomorrow."

Now, look at the Picture Word *ship* in these two sentences. In the first sentence, it conveys the image of an action. When your reader encounters it, he sees people wrapping the sails, putting them in a box, taking them to the post office, and so on.

And then look at the same Picture Word in the second sentence. Here it conveys the image of a huge object. When the reader encounters it, he sees a dock, funnels spouting steam, people on board waving good-bye, and perhaps even the tugs pulling the great ship out into the river.

So the same Picture Word conjures up two entirely different, kinds of images in your reader. They both stem from the same source, but they are now completely opposed to each other.

And you have to make sure that your reader knows which one of these images to use. This is the process of *clarification.*

Clarification means, once again, that *you have deliberately restricted every Picture Word in your sentence to a single meaning.*

Therefore, your reader cannot get another meaning out of that sentence that you did not put into it.

How do you restrict those ambiguous meanings? How do you clarify your sentences? In much the same way as you simplified them before.

Ambiguity is a tricky problem. It slips up on you when you're not looking. Therefore, you need a three-step process to eliminate it:

First, you write the sentences, trying to make them as simple and clear as you can.

Then, if possible, you leave them for a night. And then, the next morning, you come back to them cold. And you reread them again.

In this final reading, you will probably pick up ambiguities, double meanings you did not intend. Let's look at some of them now:

1.   *A Picture Word is not complete enough in itself to convey the full image.*

For example:

"When *a boy,* my father gave me his watch."

Here, the Picture Word *boy* is incomplete by itself, and therefore can be misinterpreted. At first glance it sounds like this: When the father was a boy, he gave his son-to-be his watch.

Therefore, we must eliminate this wrong meaning in the same way we did in the example above. *By adding enough ex-*

tra words (filling out the image) until it cannot be misinterpreted.

Like this:

"When *I was a boy,* my father gave me his watch."

2. *A Picture Word can be interpreted in two ways.*

For example, writers have been swindled for years by this sentence:

"Your royalty will be 10% of the price of the book." Here, the pivotal Picture Word is *price.* Because *price* has two meanings. It can mean full bookstore price. Or it can mean the price the publisher gets from the bookstore, which is usually much lower.

So there is a built-in misunderstanding in this sentence. And the rule for eliminating it is as simple as this:

Remove all meanings from your pivotal Picture Words except the one you intend. Do this by adding enough extra words till the image can be interpreted in only one way.

Thus, in the example above, you would ask that the publisher put in the additional Picture Words "the price of the book *to the customer in the store."* And the meaning then could not be misinterpreted.

3. *A Picture Word is joined to the rest of the sentence with the wrong Connector, and therefore takes on the wrong meaning.*

For example:

"Would you like to sweep the floor *with me?"*

Here the misinterpretation becomes funny. It is caused, of course, by the misuse of the otherwise-perfectly-good Connector *with.*

This misuse of *with* gives *me* in the structure of the sentence the same position that *broom* or *mop* would usually have.

Thus, a marvelously funny image comes out of the sentence at first reading.

How do you correct it? Like this:

Remove the word that is causing the misinterpretation. And replace it with the word (or words) that will give the correct image ... and only the correct image.

Like this:

"Would you like to *help me* sweep the floor?"

4.   *A Picture Word (or phrase) is misplaced in the sentence – and therefore gives the wrong image.*

For example:

"Last night Mrs. Jones was burned while cooking her husband's supper *in a terrible manner.*"

Poor Mrs. Jones! And her poor husband! Here the words are right, but their placement destroys the image they are meant to convey.

How do you correct it? With this simple rule:

Put all details as close to the main image as possible. Don't let them get separated.

In this sentence, for example, *in a terrible manner* is a detail of *burned.* Therefore, it should be placed right next to it.

The trouble was caused when the writer allowed it to wander too far back in the sentence. Thus, it came to rest next to *supper,* and seemingly became a most unfortunate detail of that.

To correct it, therefore, you revise it like this:

"Last night Mrs. Jones was burned *in a terrible manner* while cooking her husband's supper."

5. ·   *A condensing Connector does not make clear which Picture Word it refers to in the sentence in front of it.*

Like this:

"There are four different ways these mistakes may confuse your readers. *They* may obscure your meanings. *They* may ..."

As you remember, these condensing Connectors take the place, in the second sentence, of a whole image in the first.

Each of these condensing Connectors is a single word: *him, her, they, them, it* and so on. Each condenses an image in the first sentence, and carries it forth as a part of the second.

But, and this is important, the first sentence may, on occasion, have two images in it that could relate to the condensing Connector that follows in the second sentence.

In the example above, for instance, there are two entirely different Picture Words that *they* might pick up. These original images are *mistakes* and *readers*. Therefore, you have to clarify which one of them you want *they*, in the second sentence, to refer back to.

You do this by *repetition*. You repeat the original image in the second sentence, so there can be no confusion.

And your revised sentence-flow looks like this:

"There are four different ways these mistakes may confuse your readers. *Such mistakes* may obscure your meanings. They may ..."

6. *A condensing Connector may be too far separated from its prime image, and therefore not show clearly enough that it refers back to that image.*

For example:

"This is simply the carrying over of a key image from one sentence to a second sentence, and then perhaps to a third sentence, a fourth, and so on. But every time *it* is repeated, it is also expanded ..."

Here, *it* refers back to the original image, the *key image*. But it is separated from that original image by twenty-one words. And those words all convey other strong images that cause the reader to forget the original one.

So *it* is not close enough to its original image to do its job. So, to be perfectly clear, we have to pull the condensing Connector *it* out, and put back the original image, like this:

"This is simply the carrying over of a key image from one sentence to a second sentence, and then perhaps to a third sentence, a fourth, and so on. But every time *that image* is repeated, it is also expanded ..."

So there you have them. Six different types of double meanings that can make even simple sentences unclear.

When you eliminate these double meanings, when you restrict your key images to only one meaning, you have built clarity into your sentences.

And when you combine this clarity technique with the simplification techniques you have already learned, it will be impossible for your sentences to be misunderstood.

So you have now solved the understanding problem – the key problem of all grammar, and all communication. For communication, after all, is the act of transmitting your own understanding to someone else. And grammar is the collection of techniques that you use to do this.

We could stop the book at this point. But there are two other contributions that these techniques can make to your communication:

They can allow you to build wit, metaphor, symbolism and suspense (in other words, style) into your communication.

And they can allow you to develop your flow of thought more deeply and completely than you might otherwise do without them.

We'll see how in the next two chapters.

Exercises and Applications
for Chapter 8

In this chapter, we have added clarity techniques to simplicity techniques. And we have made sure that our images cannot be misunderstood, just as we previously made sure that our relationships could not be misunderstood.

So let's review again, filling in the blanks or circling the correct choices:

1. When your relationships are immediately understood by your reader, your sentences are *(simple/complicated)*.

2. And when your images are immediately understood, your sentences are *(clear/ambiguous)*.

3. You want your sentences to be clear, as well as _____.

4. To make them simple, you concentrated on your Connecting Words. And to make them _____, you concentrate on your Picture Words.

5. To make your sentences clear, you have to concentrate on the proper use of _____.

6. A Picture Word, or phrase, is _____ when it has only one possible meaning in the sentence in which it is used.

7. A Picture Word is unclear (ambiguous) when it has more than _____ meaning in that sentence. And when you did not intend it to have those extra meanings.

8. But the big problem with Picture Words is that many of them may have more than _____ meaning.

9. Some Picture Words have _____ or more meanings.

10. And they can slip back and forth between those meanings before you are even aware of it.

So the process of making a sentence clear is the process of restricting your Picture Words to only _____ meaning.

11. Clarification means that you have deliberately restricted every Picture Word in your sentence to only _____ meaning.

12.   You do this by a three-step process:

First, you write the sentence, trying to make it as simple and _____ as you can.

Second, you leave the sentence alone for a night.

13.   And third, you come back to that sentence cold the next morning. You read it again. And you check it to see if there are any Picture Words in it that are not _____.

14.   In other words, you check to see if there are any Picture Words in that sentence (or in that flow of sentences) that have more than _____ meaning.

15.   If there are, if any Picture Word has two meanings, then you simply cut out _____ of them.

16.   You cut out _____ of those meanings by adding enough words to that sentence till it can only be read in one way.

17.   You revise that sentence till that Picture Word can only have _____ meaning. And no more.

So there you have the process of clarification. That's all there is to it: *Write. Read again. And cut out double meanings.*

18.   Now let's look at some of these types of double meanings. And give you some practice in clarifying them.

As we have already seen, the first of them is the Picture Word that can be interpreted in two ways.

For example (a classic case):

"As we look at the conclusion of the 1980s and the beginning of the 1990s, we see business everywhere spilling across national boundaries and covering the globe. In no case has this been more true than for the oil industry." (From remarks made by the chairman of the board of one of the largest oil companies in the world, and reprinted in the company's house publication.)

Now, because of unplanned double meanings, this perfectly serious statement becomes funny and self-damaging.

19.   Why? Because of the combination of meanings between *oil* in the second sentence, and two Picture Words in the first sentence. They are _____ing and _____ing.

Both *spilling* and *covering* in the first sentence were intended to be used in this way: As vivid metaphors to show the way *business* was spreading across the globe.

This was their intended meaning. And it would have stood up just fine, *if* the second sentence hadn't been added to it.

20.   But it was. And therefore, the audience saw a second, unplanned meaning instead. Instead of seeing *business* spilling and covering the globe, they saw _____ spilling and covering the globe.

And so the chairman of the board unwittingly set a verbal trap for himself. He should have prepared his remarks in advance. And reread them before he spoke them.

Or, before he published them again, he should have had some unbiased editor go over them, who could pick up the double meaning.

Now, how would you correct this double meaning? The usual way, which we discussed in this chapter, is to remove the double meaning by adding extra words till the image can be interpreted in only one way.

In most cases, this works. But in this case, it does not. Why? Because here the unwanted image is just too strong to be allowed to stand in any way.

So we add an extra rule: *If the unwanted double image is too strongly fixed in your Picture Words, change one or more of them until it's removed.*

21.   In this case, then, we would probably have to take out _____ and _____.

We would have to replace them with two Picture Words that were not as visual as these. That were more abstract. And, especially, that could not be linked in a double meaning with *oil.*

22.   Can you think of any other Picture Words to use instead? If so, write your revised image here:

"... we see business everywhere _____

_____

_____

Here's my version, for comparison with your own:

"... we see business everywhere *transcending* national boundaries and *having financial commitments* across the globe."

You can see at once, of course, that I purposely put in Picture Words that brought out images of business organizations and their abstract functions. This was to allow me to use *oil* in the next sentence with no possibility of any physical-image link-up at all.

So we have taken a rather humorous ambiguity, and corrected it. We have removed the unfortunate double meanings in these Picture Words, and left our reader with only one image – one conclusion to draw.

23.   So the first point at which ambiguity can arise is with Picture Words that can have more than _____ meaning.

And we eliminate those double meanings in either of two ways:

By adding enough extra words till that image can be interpreted in only one way.

Or by removing the unfortunate Picture Words entirely. And replacing them with similar Picture Words which do not have the double meanings.

24.   And now we move on to the second type of ambiguity: A Picture Word that is not complete enough in itself to convey the full image.

For example:

"Let the baby eat herself."

Here, the Picture Word h_____ is incomplete by itself, and can therefore be misinterpreted.

25.   Therefore, we must prevent this misinterpretation by adding an extra Connector, in front of *herself,* which gives it the correct relationship to the rest of the sentence. This Connector should be: _____.

And therefore, the correct sentence reads:

"Let the baby eat by herself."

A simple clarification.

26.   Now try this one:

"Would you like to join me in a cup of coffee?"

The ambiguity here occurs between the Connector, *in*, and the phrase, _____ _____ _____
_____.

As the sentence reads now, it sounds like an invitation for a swim in an Olympic-pool-size cup of coffee.

27.   So, once again, we have to add a clarifying word. This should be the Picture Word _____*ing*.

And the corrected sentence now reads:

"Would you like to join me in having a cup of coffee?"

28.   So we go on to our next point of ambiguity: A Picture Word, or phrase, that is misplaced in the sentence, and therefore gives the wrong image.

For example:

"When he fell, Arthur struck the goldfish bowl with his head, which fortunately was empty."

Here, the phrase _____ is complete, but quite amusingly misplaced.

29.   So our clarification process here is one of movement. We simply move the offending phrase next to the Picture Word that it really describes.

And then it reads like this (write your version here):

_____

_____

Here's my version:

"When he fell, Arthur struck the goldfish bowl, which fortunately was empty, with his head."

A little awkward. But at least it is now clear.

30.   How about this one, though?

"Mr. Jones wants to buy an old bed for his wife with a brass head."

Here the misplaced phrase is: _____
_____.

31. And the corrected sentence would read like this:

_____

_____

So now we've investigated four ways that ambiguity can arise within the sentence itself. And we've seen how to clarify each one of them.

But ambiguity can also arise between two sentences. And it arises, usually, in the misuse of condensing Connectors.

As we have seen, there are two ways that these condensing Connectors can be misused:

When a condensing Connector does not make clear which Picture Word it refers to in the sentence in front of it.

Or when a condensing Connector is too far separated from its prime image, and therefore the reader cannot make the connection.

32. Both ambiguities are corrected in the same way: By replacing the Connector with a repetition of the original Picture Word.

For example:

"Put your pencil next to your test paper on the desk. And don't begin working on it till I give you the signal."

Here the ambiguous condensing Connector is _____.

33. *It* is ambiguous because it can refer to anyone of three Picture Words in the preceding sentence. These Picture Words are *p*, _____, *p* _____, and *d* _____.

34. So you correct this ambiguity by substituting the correct Picture Word in the second sentence. Like this:

"And don't begin working on your _____ till I give you the signal."

Once again, the process is the same as for all other clarifications: Write the sentence. Leave it alone for a while. Then check it again to pick up ambiguities. And correct them as we've learned here.

That's all there is to clarification. It is a powerful tool, and yet extremely simple to use.

Combine it with simplification, and your reader must understand your sentences the moment she encounters them. As we have said before, these two tools enable you to lick the understanding problem.

But there are also several delightful side benefits of these clarification insights. And now let's go on to put them to work.

Chapter 9

How to Use the Clarity Principle to Build Wit, Symbolism, and Suspense into Your Writing

NOW LET'S ADD even more spice to your communication. We do it by "twisting" the clarity principle we discovered in the last chapter.

As you remember, that clarity principle went like this:

Clarity depends on Picture Words. If the Picture Words in your sentence have only one possible meaning, they are clear.

And so, to clarify ambiguous sentences, restrict each of your Picture Words to only one possible meaning.

But there is another way to use this principle. Just as deliberately. But in exactly the opposite direction, to give us an entirely different range of effects.

Here, instead of using the clarity principle to restrict our Picture Words to a single meaning, we deliberately use it to give our key words two simultaneous meanings or more.

And we use these two simultaneous meanings to gain wit, or symbolism, or suspense.

Let's see how we do this:

First of all, as we have seen before, a great many Picture Words are capable of two or more meanings. Perhaps, to begin with, each of them had only one meaning. But, as they were used over the centuries in the language, they picked up a second meaning. And perhaps a third. And even more.

Thus, these words come to you with an inventory of meanings already attached to them. They have multiple meanings. And these multiple meanings are both a peril and an opportunity.

They are perilous because they open up the possibility of ambiguity, and thus misunderstanding. But we have already seen how to correct this.

On the other hand, each of them presents you with an opportunity. Because you can deliberately build two of these meanings into a sentence, to give that sentence a punch it would never have had without them.

So let's give these multiple meaning words a special title. Let's call them *Pivot Words,* because they allow you to pivot from one meaning to another in your sentence. And let's explore the three main types of pivots they can give you.

The first is *wit.* We can define it in this way:

Wit is the humorous change in a Pivot Word, in mid-image, from one meaning to another.

For example, let's take Robert Benchley's famous remark: "I can't wait to get out of these wet clothes, and into a dry martini."

Where, in this sentence, is the wit? In the last image, of course. It is contained in the last two Picture Words, *dry martini.*

But what makes these two words witty? The simple fact that the author has tricked us. He has built up an expectation in our minds, and then shattered it in mid-image. And, by so doing, he has thrown us into an entirely different, and quite funny, new meaning.

The expectation is based on these two sets of parallel phrases:

get out of ... and into

wet ... dry

First of all, when we *get out of* one kind of thing, we usually expect to get *into* something similar. Thus, when we get out of *street clothes,* we expect to get into a *bathrobe,* or *pajamas,* or perhaps even *bed.*

Secondly, in exactly the same way, when we use the Picture Word *wet* to mean *soaked in water,* we usually expect *dry* to mean *devoid of water.*

But it does not mean *devoid of water* here. And this is the trick. And the source of the wit.

It is the shift, in mid-image, of the meaning of the word "dry" that catches us unawares. And then startles us. And then makes us laugh.

And it is this deliberate double meaning that constitutes the wit we appreciate so much here.

But you can do the same thing. Once you see the source of this wit, you can start seeking out such Pivot Words too. And you can begin putting them in sentences that cause them to shift from one meaning to another with both shock and laughter.

Like these:

The Harvard Repertory Company *played* Hamlet last night. Hamlet *lost.*

If all the young ladies at this Prom were *laid* end to end, I wouldn't be surprised.

How do you *like* children, Mr. Fields"? "Well-cooked."

A man *wrapped up* in himself makes a small package.

Anthropology is the study of man *embracing* woman. You can see each of the meaning-shifts in the italicized words:

Played goes from *giving a performance* to *competing in a game.*

Laid goes from *being placed on the ground* to *being made love to.*

Like goes from *relating affectionately to* to *having a preference in food.*

Wrapped up goes from *intensely concerned with* to *being placed in a package.*

And *embracing* goes from *dealing with as its subject matter* to *putting one's arms around.* And it is this *shift in meaning,* in mid-image, that comprises *wit.*

It is the first valuable stylistic effect that the clarity principle can give you.

The second is closely related to it. It is also humorous. But it depends not so much on a shift in meaning, as a blend of meanings.

It is called the *pun*. It *works by taking a familiar statement, and replacing its Pivot Word by another word which sounds about the same, but which has a different meaning.*

Thus, the new sentence – the pun – gives you two meanings. You get the meaning of the original statement. And you get the meaning of the new statement. And the contrast between the two yields the fun.

For example:

"Thanks for the *mammaries.*"

Here the original statement was, "Thanks for the *memories.*" *Mammaries* sounds like *memories,* and is used to replace it. It is therefore the Pivot Word. And it yields the comparison of *"Memories of mammaries,"* which is as much fun as the original pun itself.

Here, again, we have a double meaning used deliberately to give a desired effect. The process in both cases is the same. But a different kind of meaning was chosen, to give a different effect.

Let's review the process. And the kinds of effects we've already gotten from it:

First, *clarity* results when we restrict a Pivot Word to only one meaning.

Ambiguity results when a Pivot Word has more than one meaning, and there is no way for our reader to choose between them.

Wit results when we deliberately shift, in mid-image, a Pivot Word from one meaning to another.

And a *Pun* results when we replace one Pivot Word with another that sounds the same, and let their two meanings interact with each other.

Which leads us to our next deliberate double meaning. This process has several names, depending on how many words or images it embraces in your writing.

If it is contained within one word, it is usually called

metaphor. If it uses several words or images, it is called *symbolism.* If it uses whole paragraphs or pages or episodes, it is called *allegory.*

In any case, it is the same process. That of *building two mutually reinforcing meanings into the same word or image.*

Metaphor is the simplest use of this process. It consists of taking a Picture Word, which has been used traditionally to yield a certain meaning, and using that word in a sentence which expands that meaning beyond that traditional usage.

For example:

"The ship *plowed* ahead."

Here the Picture Word *plow* has been given a double meaning, deliberately, based upon its usual meaning of *to turn earth over with a knifelike instrument.*

This original meaning still holds in this sentence. But instead of *earth* we have the *water.* And instead of a *knifelike instrument,* we have the *prow of the ship.*

So the literal meaning no longer fully holds. And a new related meaning, based on it, comes into being.

The meaning of the Pivot Word *plow* has been enlarged. So little so that we hardly notice it. And we use it again and again, to add its original meaning to dozens of new situations where it fits.

Like this:

"The quarterback spun around and handed the ball to the fullback, who *plowed* through the line for ten yards."

This process of creating *metaphors* – of adding *new, reinforcing meanings to old Picture Words* – is the way our language grows. It enables you to pile much more image, much more meaning, much more emotion into all your communications.

Again, it's a process of squeezing two meanings – two reinforcing meanings – out of a single Pivot Word.

But you can carry this process even further. You can attempt to produce two or more reinforcing meanings, not only out of single words, but also out of entire images. Out of whole sets of words.

For example, at the turn of the century, William Jennings

Bryan used this process to coin a slogan that was repeated all over America:

"You shall not crucify mankind on a cross of gold."

Now, Bryan was arguing a political issue: Whether America should go off the gold standard, or stay on it. A literal statement of this issue would have been as dry as dust. So he used this process of *reinforcing double images* – which we call *symbolism* – to make his point unforgettable.

To do this, he took the familiar Christian image of Christ crucified on the cross. He used this as his base image. And then he substituted mankind for Christ. And he made the cross of gold.

Thus, the two images echo each other. They vibrate. They resonate. All sorts of levels of meaning emerge.

And you can do the same, once you're familiar with the process. Our language is full of such basic images. They come from the Bible, mythology, folk tales, history – all the common images we share with each other.

These images may be used in a single sentence, as Bryan has used his crucifixion image above. Or they may be spread out over a series of sentences.

Or they may comprise an entire story or book, as they do in James Joyce's *Ulysses*. When they become this extensive, then the series of reinforcing double images that comprises them may be called *allegory*.

So we have a whole range of reinforcing double meanings. Contained in a single word, they are called a *metaphor*. Spread out over a series of words, or images, they are called *symbolism*. And serving as the backbone for an entire story, they are called *allegory*.

Thus, grammar imperceptibly blends into literature. The same mechanisms that create fine sentences also create fine stories. The fundamental rules carry you from your first word to your finished book.

And now we come to the last effect that this clarity principle can give you – *suspense*.

Suspense can be defined as *planned ambiguity*. As the process of *deliberately leaving the reader unsure of some vital element in your thought-flow*.

For example, every gossip creates suspense in his listener when he says:

"*Who* do you think was seen last night with Sarah's husband?"

Pivot Word here is *who*. It is meant to be ambiguous. To grip the listener. To secure his attention until the ambiguity is cleared up by the next statement.

And great writers use the same device. For example, this opening for a short story:

"Don't turn around or I'll blow off your head."

Here, everything is left deliberately ambiguous: Who is speaking. Who is being spoken to. What the setting is. Everything except the threatening statement, designed deliberately to force the reader into the next sentence, to discover what is happening.

So even ambiguity can have its value, if it is *planned ambiguity*. The creation of deliberate *suspense*.

So there you have them. We started with the clarity principal. We explored various twists on that principle. And we came up with *wit ... puns ... metaphors ... symbolism ... allegory ...* and *suspense* to your writing.

Once again, the use of such devices adds *style* to your writing. They win friends and influence people. They can express deep emotions or subtle fun.

They add spice to your communication. They heighten, rather than detract from its overall clarity. They show instantly that you can master words, and combinations of words, and the many different effects they can give.

Yet they all derive from specialized uses of your Picture Words. They are the frosting on the cake of your thought. And now let's turn to the main body of that thought. And, as our last step in the communication process, see how to develop that thought from beginning to end.

**Exercises and Applications
for Chapter 9**

In these exercises, either fill in the blank or circle the correct choice.

We have now explored the marvelous effects that Pivot Words (and Pivot Ideas) can give you. They are, as you remember:

Wit...

Puns...

Metaphors...

Symbolism...

Allegory...

Suspense...

Six wonderful ways to make your communication deeper, broader and far more beautiful for your reader.

1.   And they all come from a simple insight: That there are certain Picture Words in our language – called *Pivot Words* – that have more than _____ meaning.

2.   And we can use these multiple meanings – consciously and deliberately – to gain any of these effects.

What we do, to accomplish this, is simply plan our double meaning. We seek out our deliberate d _____ meanings, and we use them to amuse, or disturb, or stimulate our reader's mind.

3.   The first of these double-meaning effects is *wit.* And wit, as we have seen, can be defined as follows:

Wit is the humorous change in a P_____ W_____ from one meaning to another in mid-sentence.

4.   Most wit, of course, is deliberate. But there is also a great deal of "unconscious wit" in everyday speech.

Slips of the tongue, for example, make us laugh by unconsciously changing image in mid-sentence, just as deliberate wit does.

We have a marvelous example of this in exercise 24 from the last chapter. There, as you remember, we encountered this awkward sentence:

"Would you like to join me in a cup of coffee?"

This is unintentional humor. The speaker did not know he was being funny. And yet, this slip of the tongue uses exactly the same Pivot Word structure as Robert Benchley's carefully-worked-out remark in this chapter:

"I can't wait to get out of these wet clothes, and into a dry martini."

So the "witty" person is the person who uses – deliberately – the image-changes that other people use only haphazardly.

And what we are trying to do here is build that "deliberateness" into your communication. We can only do this, of course, by increasing your awareness of the process of wit. By training you to recognize opportunities for wit.

We cannot do it by giving you a list of "witty" Pivot Words. And then asking you to mechanically apply them to conversations 1 ... 2 ... 3 ... and so forth.

Wit doesn't work that way. To be good, it has to be spontaneous. It has to fit the occasion.

Wit is a matter of opportunity. Of knowing the process of creating wit so well that you almost automatically slip in the image-change when the conversational opening occurs.

So, in order to build into you this awareness, and this ability to shift image, let's look at the wit of several famous people. And then analyze how they did it.

5.   Let's start with one of the wittiest men of all time – Oscar Wilde. Here is one of his most famous remarks:

"Thirty-five is a very attractive age. London society is full of women of the very highest birth who have, of their own free choice, remained thirty-five for years."

Here, of course, the Pivot Word is _____-_____.

The first time it is used here, *thirty-five* means *the chronological age of a person*. The second time it is used, however, *thirty-five* means *the stated age of a person*.

It is the difference in these two meanings – the shift in meaning from one to another – that constitutes the surprise here, the kick, and the wit.

Here, then, meaning-shift equals wit.

6.   But meaning-shift can be used much more subtly than this. And Wilde is a master at doing it. For example, in this famous line:

"Life is much too important a thing to ever talk seriously about it."

Now I'm sure you can see the meaning-shift here at a glance. It takes place, not in a single Pivot Word, but in two. In the contradiction between the accepted meaning of *important* and the accepted meaning of s_____.

We tend automatically to assume that something that is *important* must also be *serious.* Wilde says No. And in so doing, tricks us into a deeper understanding.

7.   Now let's move from the nineteenth century to the twentieth. And see how another great English wit, George Bernard Shaw, uses the same device of meaning-shift to achieve his effect. Like this:

"My way of joking is to tell the truth. It's the funniest joke in the world."

Here, again, contradiction is used as a weapon of wit. The Pivot Word here is t _____.

8.   And the contradiction is attained by equating, in the second sentence, this *truth* with a _____.

We don't expect it. It startles us. And, consequently, makes us think more deeply.

9.   Now let us shift from England to America, and from men of letters to men of action. In fact, to presidents.

Let us start with Abraham Lincoln. And see, from his examples, how wit can be used to add sharpness to command.

We begin with a telegram of reprimand, to General G. B. McClellan:

"I have just read your dispatch about sore-tongued and

fatigued horses.

Will you pardon me for asking what the horses of your army have done since the battle of Antietam that fatigues anything?"

The Pivot Word here, which is repeated in both sentences, is, of course, _____.

10.   And now, the use of wit to spur action. In a telegram from Lincoln to a different breed of general, Ulysses S. Grant, in April 1865:

"General Sheridan says, 'If the thing is pressed, I think Lee will surrender.' Let the thing be pressed."

The Pivot Word here is _____.

The meaning-shift here is one of emphasis: The demand that a potential situation be converted into an actuality.

Notice, incidentally, how incredibly strong the use of wit here makes this short command. Lincoln could not have phrased it as powerfully with a hundred more words.

Where does this power come from? From the fact that wit – like other forms of humor – is completed, not on the page, but in the reader's mind.

Here, for example, Lincoln sets up the meaning-shift with his repetition of the Picture Word *pressed*. But he lets Grant complete it. He lets Grant derive the final meaning himself. He does not tell Grant to intensify the attack. He *implies* it. He makes certain that the logic of his statements will cause the idea of intensification to occur in Grant's mind. And the command gains great electricity by the very fact that it is left incomplete on paper, to be completed by Grant.

11.   Now, as a final example, let's shift again – to our own time – and to Jack Kennedy. Kennedy knew very well the cutting edge of wit. But he also used it continuously to kid himself. To make himself more human and likable to the country he represented.

For example, almost immediately after being elected, he said this at a Washington testimonial dinner:

"When we got into office, the thing that surprised me

most was to find out that things were just as bad as we'd been saying they were."

The Pivot Word here concerns Kennedy's discovery that his own campaign claims were true. It is the Picture Word, su _____, working in conjunction with the phrase, to *"find out that things were just as bad as we were saying they were."*

12.   So, wit is our first Pivot-Word effect. Our second is the *pun.*

As you remember, *puns* are created by taking a familiar statement, and replacing a P_____ W_____ in that statement with another word which sounds just about the same, but which has a different meaning.

13.   So let's look at a few puns. And analyze how they were put together.

Here's one used by Lawrence Durrell, the fine contemporary English writer. Supposedly, it was asked of one gourmet by another:

"Is there a life beyond the gravy?"

Yes, it hurts. All puns hurt a little. That's why some people call them "the lowest form of wit. "Although others (such as Marshall McLuhan) consider them the highest form.

In any case, the Pivot Word here is _____.

14.   And the original word, from which it takes off, is

_____.

15.   So, from *Is there a life beyond the grave,* we go to *Is there a life beyond the gravy.* You can see the shift in meaning: From the profound to the trivial.

And you can see how the two meanings resonate – how they continually play in and out of each other as you keep comparing them back and forth.

This is why so very many intellectuals love puns – because they dredge up so many levels of meaning simultaneously.

Here's another one from the food field:

"What a friend we have in cheeses."

Here, the Pivot Word is _____.

16.   And the original word, from which it takes off, is

_____.

The shift in meaning is from the religious to the trivial.

17.   Now let's shift jeers, and look at two of the most profound users of puns today – James Joyce and Marshall McLuhan.

McLuhan, in discussing the fantastic growth rate of Japan today, used this one:

"Goodness Geishas me!"

Here, the Pivot Word is _____.

18.   And the old Picture Word it replaces is _____.

19.   And Joyce topped him with this one, from *Finnegans Wake:*

"I never open me mouth but I put me feed in it."

20.   Here, the Pivot Word is _____.

21.   And the older Picture Word it replaces is _____.

If you think about it for a minute, you can see the vibrating levels of meaning that come out of such a simple shift as this.

22.   And, like all stylistic devices, puns have practical uses, as well as purely decorative ones.

For example, in a debate, Prime Minister Trudeau of Canada was asked:

"Aren't you some kind of a communist?"

To which he replied:

"No, I'm a canoeist."

End of debate. Point won. Crowd pleased. Opponent demolished. All because Trudeau understood what the shift in meaning between _____ and _____ could do in a situation of this kind.

23.   So, now we've explored puns. And we can go on to our third Pivot Word device, the *metaphor.*

Our language, of course, is incredibly rich in metaphors, and coins them all the time. This, once again, is the way it grows.

A metaphor is created by taking a Picture Word, which has been traditionally used to yield a certain meaning,

and using that word in a sentence which expands that m
_____ beyond that traditional usage.

Once again, most people think of metaphors as literary devices. Which they are, of course. But they are also immensely practical tools for everyday business and social life.

Why? Because they can sting people's minds. Expand their awareness. Cause them to think of problems and opportunities in different terms. And make news doing it.

24.   For example, this quote from the *New York Times:*

"Psychoanalysis is vanishing," says Dr. Szasz. "The bark is still there, but the molars are gone."

The punch of this statement rests on two Pivot Words: b _____ and m _____. They bring up the metaphorical image of a dog who has grown old, and can only warn, but no longer hurt.

25.   Advertising is one of the richest sources of new metaphor. For example, this ad by the Young and Rubicam ad agency for itself:

"A winning smile becomes a winning commercial when the selling message has teeth in it."

Here, the metaphor starts off with *smile*. And then surprises us with a twist at the end when the Pivot Word, _____, is suddenly brought in.

In this sentence, metaphor and wit merge. The result is punch – impact – attention. The kind of attention that creates fortunes.

Notice the simplicity and shortness of these sentences. And yet their enormous power. More proof that, in communication as well as in surgery, a scalpel is better than a sledgehammer.

26.   But it's important to remember, too, that metaphor –as well as wit – can make us laugh. Returning to Oscar Wilde again, we find:

"Women give to men the very gold of their lives. But they invariably want it back in small change."

Here, the metaphor begins in the first sentence with the Picture Word g _____. And then surprises us at the end of the second sentence with a further twist in metaphor, contained in s _____ c _____.

27.   At this point, when metaphor is piled upon metaphor, we are coming close to our next Pivot Word device: *Symbolic discourse.*

Here, we have a series of reinforcing double images – one after the other – that may go on for pages, or even entire chapters or books.

For example, this moving passage from George Bernard Shaw's *Saint Joan* (when Joan is being condemned to the stake by her captors).

JOAN. I know your counsel is of the devil, and that mine is of God.

JUDGE. You wicked girl: If your counsel were of God would He not deliver you?

JOAN. His ways are not your ways. He wills that I go through the fire to his bosom; for I am His child, and you are not fit that I should live among you. That is my last word to you.

Here, again, simplicity is combined with style to produce great profundity. Joan's last speech abounds in metaphors: *Fire ... bosom ... child.* All of which add great poetry and depth of feeling to her simple words.

So we have seen – with the use of *wit, puns, metaphors,* and *symbolism* – how to add surprise and laughter and depth and power to our simplest statements.

Suspense and *allegory* also work on the same Pivot Word mechanism that we have already explored in these exercises. They are simply more elaborate than the examples we have considered.

So we have finished with the devices of adding style to our individual sentences. Now we go on to our final step: To unify these sentences into a complete and coherent overall discourse.

Chapter 10

Elaboration –
How to Develop
Your Flow of Thought
From Sentence to Sentence

S O LET US now take one last review. And then go on to our final step in the process from grammar to communication .

Both grammar and communication are concerned with one goal: To transfer your thoughts into other people's minds .

What you wish to transfer, however, is not just a single thought, but complete flows of thought. Thought-flows as complicated, for example, as a novel, or a business report.

To accomplish this transfer, you divide that flow of thought into several different, but overlapping steps.

First, as we have seen, you compose each individual sentence.

Then you link each pair of sentences together.

And then (but actually at the same time) you take your *core ideas* – the ideas you really want your reader to understand – *and you develop each one of them in the stream of sentences.*

This is the process of *elaboration.* And we shall spend this chapter studying it.

Here is how it works:

We will assume that you introduce your reader to your first core idea in your first sentence. Let's start with the simplest possible example, and the one we know best: *Harry.*

As you remember, our first sentence about poor old Harry went like this:

"Yesterday, I hit Harry."

Here, in this first sentence, you have expressed your first core idea that you *hit* Harry.

Now, you have chosen this core idea deliberately. You knew that it was out of the ordinary. That it was shocking. That it would grab your listener's attention immediately.

Her mind is now focused on the fact that you suddenly hit Harry. She wants to know why? How? With what result?

She is ready for more detail. For your next sentence. For the further development of this "startling" thought.

So you go on, to give her the elaboration she now wants. Like this:

"I *hit* him because he is a low-down, miserable son of a gun. I *hit* him because I was at my wit's end, and I decided that I no longer cared about the consequences.

"I *hit* him till he fell down. And then he begged me to stop. And then I walked away."

Now, let's look at this stream of sentences, and pick up the following information from them:

1.   What is the core idea?
2.   How is it elaborated?
3.   How is it summarized, or terminated?
4.   How is it transferred (or bridged, or connected) to the next core idea?

Here are the answers to these questions:

1.   As we have seen, the first core idea is the fact that you have *hit* Harry. It is a startling action, unexpected by your listener, and therefore capable of riveting his attention.

2. This core idea is elaborated, in the second and third sentences, in this way: *By giving your motives for doing it.* These motives are:

because he is a low-down, miserable son of a gun ...

because I was at my wit's end...

and *because* I decided that I no longer cared about the consequences.

There are thus three motives. I have italicized the Connectors that tie them in to the core idea.

As you can see, all of them are reasons-why. In the first two images, the Connector *because* shows this reason-why relationship to your reader. In the third image, it is implied by the Connector *and,* and sentence-structure expectation.

3.   But the use of *and* in the third image also performs another task for us here. It also signals the reader that you are through giving her the reasons why you hit Harry. That you are through with this second core idea.

Thus, she knows that you are now ready to pass on to your next core idea.

4.   And you do this in the next sentence: *I hit him till he fell down.*

Here, you repeat your first core idea, *hit,* which is an action. Then you transfer it to a second action, *fell.* And you bridge the two actions by the Connector, *till.*

Thus, in this sentence, you have switched from the motives for an action to the continuation of that action. You are now leading your reader into a straight *narrative sequence,* showing her *what happened next.*

This narrative sequence is then continued in the next two sentences:

"And then he begged me to stop. And then I walked away."

Now you have given your reader two further actions - *begged* and *walked.* And the Connecting Words that bridge these two actions, that tie them in to the rest of the thought-flow, are *and then* and *and then.*

So, in these three paragraphs, you developed at least three core ideas. In the first paragraph, you stated an action. In the second paragraph, you gave your reasons for doing it. And in the third paragraph, you told your reader what happened next.

And you used linking Connectors as bridges each step of the way. And you also used the condensing Connectors *him* and *he,* so your listener would be sure to remember that it was old Harry that you were hitting all the way.

This, then, is our first example of the process of *elaboration*. The process of *developing your flow of thought, from sentence to sentence.*

And the general rule for this elaboration process is simply this:

Choose a core idea. Tell your listener all the details he has to know about it, in as many sentences as this takes. Then connect that core idea on to the next core idea. And then go on from there.

So *elaboration* involves these three steps:

- Choosing your core idea.
- Choosing the way you want to elaborate it.
- And choosing the way you're going to bridge it into your next core idea.

In fact, writing, or speaking, or communication of any kind can be considered a continually developing stream of elaborations. And each of these elaborations may consist of one or more sentences.

So – just as you have already built words into images, and then into sentences – now you can build sentences into elaborations.

Each of these elaborations takes a core idea, and tells your reader as much about it as you think he has to know. And then it bridges in to the next core idea.

Now, we can give a name to this *change from one core idea to another.* We can call it *change of focus.*

This name is a metaphor, of course. It comes from the movies. From that moment, for example, when the camera *changes focus* from a close-up to a long-shot.

Before that moment, the movie viewer has seen one kind of picture. After it, she sees another. The continuity of the scene continues, but she is now watching it from another viewpoint.

We can do the same thing in verbal communication, in talking or writing. When we shift from one core idea to another, we change focus. *And we should express that change in focus by beginning a new paragraph.*

Now, what is a paragraph? It is *the second arbitrary division – the second arbitrary resting place – between your two fundamental kinds of words, and your complete flow of thought.*

The first resting place, of course, is the sentence. Its function is to provide your reader with a place to rest, after he has absorbed as much of your thought as he is capable of at one time.

The length of any sentence, therefore, is arbitrary. This means that it has an upper limit, but not a bottom one. And that there is a whole range of choices available to you in between these two limits.

The upper limit, of course, is fixed by the maximum amount of detail that any reader can understand at one time. As we have seen in the chapters on simplification, if you exceed this limit, you lose or confuse him.

But, as we have also seen, there is a huge range of choice available below that upper limit. It can go all the way down to one or two words.

And you can choose from that range as you please. It doesn't matter how long or short that sentence is, as long as it:

- is immediately understandable;
- has, if possible, a pleasant effect (style);
- and develops and elaborates on your flow of thought, as it picks that flow of thought up from the sentences in front of it.

And exactly the same procedures work for paragraphs. Just as sentences are collections of words, so paragraphs are collections of sentences. And just as sentences have an upper limit (understandably), so paragraphs have an upper limit (focus).

In other words, *a paragraph should be no longer than the number of sentences it takes to elaborate one core idea.*

When you shift from one core idea to the next, you should also shift into a new paragraph.

Take the *Harry* example above. Its first core idea was *hit.* This was simple and needed no elaboration .

So you went on to the second core idea – the *reasons why* Harry was hit. And you started a second paragraph for these reasons-why.

It took two sentences to list these reasons-why. Both of these sentences were contained in your second paragraph.

Then you were through with the reasons-why, and wanted to go on to your next core idea – the *narrative sequence* of what happened next. So you started a third paragraph to show this.

And this third paragraph took three sentences. But they all continued the same narrative sequence.

Had you wanted to give more detail to each of these narrative steps, however, you might have given each of them a separate paragraph. In this case, you would have made the change in focus the transition from one action to the next.

So change in focus is arbitrary. You choose it. You choose the point where you want to shift from one viewpoint to another. Just as you have already chosen how long, or how short, you want your sentences to be.

And you make those paragraphs shorter, or longer, to achieve all these effects:

Greater simplicity – if you are dealing with a complicated process that requires a number of short, separated steps.

Emphasis on certain thoughts – which can be made to stand out if they have their own paragraphs.

Avoidance of monotony – interspersing long paragraphs with short ones.

Style – for example if you wish your style to be characterized by short simple paragraphs, with lots of white space between them. This is what I do.

So there you have paragraphing. *One core idea and its elaboration – one paragraph.* Don't overload your paragraphs any more than you do your sentences.

Now, how many ways are there of elaborating these core ideas? Are there elaboration-structures, just as there were simplification-structures?

The answer, of course, is yes. We have already seen two of them in the *Harry* example above. They are: *Reasons-why.* And *narrative sequence* (or story line).

The first is an extremely limited line of elaboration. The second is almost infinitely expandable. Let us, therefore, start with it.

1.   *Narrative sequence* is the most common elaboration-structure in our language. Every story, every novel, every movie makes use of it.

It is simply the technique of taking an actor, and putting him through a series of actions in time. The actions follow one after another. And as they do, your reader learns more about your actor, and your story.

The time sequence provides the structure for your story. If you follow it exactly, you will have no trouble in organizing your thought-flow. If you violate it (by flashbacks, for example), then you must signal your reader in advance that you are doing so.

There is no need to give an example here. Any good novel or short story will give you the idea.

2.   *Reasons-why.* This elaboration-structure, like all the rest to follow, is much more limited, and cannot be used to organize an entire thought-flow. Instead, it organizes part of a thought-flow, and then gives way to another elaboration-structure.

As we have seen above, *reasons-why* are both a person's motives for doing something, and the reasons why something is so. In a narrative, such as the one about Harry, they usually come after the action. They tell why it was done. And then they give way, usually, to the next action.

3.   *Causes for an event.* This elaboration-structure is closely related to the reasons-why. But it differs from it in that it deals with objective events, rather than personal feelings.

When you report that something of importance has happened, your reader would like to know why it has happened. If you want him to gain an understanding of the event, your job then is to give him its causes in as simple and clear and direct a manner as possible.

Something like this:

"The recent stock market crash was caused by the following factors:

"1.   Tight money. Which limited the funds available for corporate expansion.

"2. Declining earnings in various former 'growth areas' of the economy.

"3. A subsequent collapse of investor confidence in a perpetual growth economy ..."

And so on. Notice that the elaboration-structure here is merged with the simplest possible form of presentation. In the first sentence, for example, the reader is signaled that the causes are to come. And each cause is given its own separate paragraph. And each paragraph is numbered.

Thus, a complicated series of causes is made simple through the techniques we learned in Chapter 6.

And then, once all the pertinent causes have been listed, you may then, if you wish, pass on to:

4. *Effects of an event.* This shows what happened because of the event. It shows the effects in the future of the event, just as the causes showed its growth in the past.

And, once again, it should be presented as simply as possible, something like this:

"As a result of the crash, the following effects were felt by the economic community:

"1. The immense profits made by Wall Street suddenly stopped.

"2. Public offerings of stock for new and untried firms dried up.

"3. Price-earnings ratios (the evaluation of future earnings by the market) were drastically reduced..."

And so on. Here again, the simplest possible structure is used to present this rather complicated material.

5. *How an event unfolds.* This is not a presentation of the causes or effects. It is, rather, the appearance of the event as it has unfolded itself at the moment.

Like this:

"The first faint warnings of the impending decline were felt in December of 1968. At that moment the Dow-Jones Index topped out, at 988.

"Month after month thereafter, it slipped lower and lower – moderately at first. But then, in January 1970, the rate of decline steepened. And a growing gloom, and then panic set in..."

And so on. Here the words serve as a movie camera, seeing only the surface of the event. They do not probe beneath the surface, just as description of a person does not probe beneath her surface appearance, or examine her motives.

6.   *Contrast.* Here you show the difference between the core idea you are describing now, and another one. Like this:

"How different were these dismal months from the holiday mood of the late sixties.

"Then, stock prices climbed almost every month. Old standbys increased by half their value in a year. Growth companies shot up four and five times. New issues often trebled the very first day they were offered to the public..."

And so on. One idea – or situation – or person – or event – set against another. So that both stand out more clearly.

7.   *Example.* Here you go from the general to the specific. From principle to application. From abstract to concrete.

To do this, you slow down the pace, and fill in the detail. Like this:

"Perhaps the perfect example of this catastrophic change is Ling-Temco-Vought. When it first came out in 1963, it traded at 3. In the ensuing years it climbed to 35 ... 46 ... 67 ... 109 ... 132 ... and finally, without pause, to 168.

"Then came the panic, and it began its long downward slide. Millions upon millions of dollars of value simply evaporated away from it. Until finally, on May 15, 1970, it closed at 6 1/4 ..."

And so on. You can, at this point, continue with other examples. Or shift back to the overall view of the event. Or go back to its causes, or its effects.

At this moment, or at any moment, several elaboration strategies are open to you. You can pick and choose as you want.

8.   *Documentation.* This is the process of bringing in proof to your thought-flow. This proof may consist of quotations from respected authorities. Or statistics or other figures. Or tests.

Usually they are simply reproduced within your thought-flow. Like this:

"Was this slump as disastrous as that of 1929? Just listen to the words of the nationally respected economist John Kenneth Galbraith: ... " And then you would reproduce Mr. Galbraith's words as he spoke them. Or, if you wish, abridge them to give the heart of their meaning to your reader as quickly as possible.

9.   *Instruction.* This is the process of teaching someone how to do something. It consists of presenting a number of steps, one after another, so that a task may be completed correctly from beginning to end.

It is most conveniently addressed to a second person, *you.* Therefore, since after the first sentence the actor is always the same, there is no need to repeat the word *you,* for each step. Instead, you can start each step with its proper action.

Certain obvious rules should be followed, but usually are not:

- Each step should be made as small as possible.
- Each step should be in the proper order.
- All steps should be included.
- The proper Connectors should be used between each step.
- The goal of the process should be mentioned at the beginning. And it should be mentioned again at the end, so the reader knows that he has arrived at it.

For example:

"Most people do not know how to open a book. Here is the right way:

"First, take the book in your hands, and open the front and back covers till they are parallel with the binding.

"Then close the book again. Then take the first ten pages, and bend them out till they are parallel with the binding.

"Then take the last ten pages. And bend them out in the opposite direction till they are parallel with the binding ... "

And so on. As you can see, instruction is the art of visual writing. Your images should be of concrete detail. Your reader should see the images in them as clearly as if you were drawing her a series of sketches.

10. *Explanation.* This is the process of telling someone how something works. It is, in essence, a series of causes. This causes this, which causes this, which causes this. And so on.

It is best done as a series of small, simple, logical steps. The same rules for instruction follow here, though in this case you are talking about a third object or event, instead of your reader.

Again, the right Connectors are essential. If your reader doesn't understand the relationships between the steps, he can't understand how one causes the other.

Here is an ordinary example:

"Here is how a camera works:

"First of all, it has a lens. A lens is a piece of specially constructed glass that lets light in from the outside world to the inside of the camera.

"On the inside of the camera, at its very back, is a roll of film. This film changes when light from the lens hits it. And, when that light hits it, it reproduces the exact scene that the lens sees, right on the film.

"So you point the camera at a scene you want to capture - let us say, the face of your child. And then you let the light from that scene come through the lens into the camera. And that light falls on the film. And the film changes. And you have the face of your child, captured forever on that film ..."

And so on. Notice how important the Connectors are. Notice how important repetition of the main elements is. Notice how important simplification is, and the breaking up of the overall process into the smallest possible number of steps.

Notice also how explanation incorporates many other elaboration structures within itself. It uses description, cause, effect, narrative sequence, example, and especially the next elaboration structure:

11. *Definition.* This is the process of introducing the new in terms of the familiar. It is one of the most important of the elaboration structures. It has great bearing upon the simplicity and clarity of your thought-flow. You will use it over and over again. So let us examine it again in some detail here.

Definition is required in two circumstances. First, when you are using a word that your reader has never encountered before. And second, when you are using a common word in a new way.

In either case, your reader must know the meaning of that word, or she cannot understand what you have to say. And you must state that meaning in words and images that she already understands.

So you must *take the new, and rephrase it for her in terms of the old.* This is the process of *definition.*

Its structure is simple. It revolves around the identity-Connector *is.*

To define a new word, you set it in front of *is.* And then, on the other side of *is,* you put a series of old words. Words the reader is already familiar with.

Thus, the definition-structure looks like this:

A *is* B plus C plus D plus E.

For example:

"A lens is a piece of specially constructed glass that lets light in from the outside world to the inside of the camera."

The term *lens* is new. It is a technical term. The reader has not encountered it before. Therefore, it must be related for her to something familiar.

She already knows *glass*. Therefore, you tell her that it is a special kind of glass. This gives her a familiar image that she can visualize, that her mind can start with.

And then you tell her how this piece of glass is special. Because it *lets light in from the outside world to the inside of the camera.*

All these words she is familiar with too. Now she knows that it is a piece of glass. And she knows why it is different from other pieces of glass.

Thus, you have taken her from the unfamiliar to the familiar. From the new to the old. From the threatening to the comfortable.

Sometimes, however, just one word will do this complete job. For example:

"Sleazy is grimy. Or dirty. Or filthy."

Here, you are defining by using synonyms – old words that mean the same thing as the new word.

Of course, some new words need a great deal of definition. It may take whole paragraphs, or even a whole book, to define them.

In that case, their definition will incorporate other elaboration structures within it. It may include description, definition, explanation, and all the rest.

But always try to keep your first definition as simple as possible. Give your reader as fast a definition-picture as possible in your first definition-sentence. And then, when he has a general idea of what the word means, go on to fill in more detail as you need it.

In any case, when he has made the connection between the new word and the old word or words, when he has his clear image of that new word, your job is done. Your reader should now be able to recognize the new word anywhere, and pull out that image immediately, the moment he encounters it.

12. *Definition – being like something else.* We use this form of definition every day, to let other people know that something that just happened *felt* like something else, or *seemed* like something else.

This is not dictionary definition. It is not a fixed, universal definition, but a new, personal, spontaneous definition. Later, if it is powerful enough, it may pass into our dictionaries, as slang does so often. But, at this time, it is in the *like* stage, rather than the *is* stage.

Its structure is the same as the *is* definition. "A is *like* B."

For example: "Running a country is *like* running a marriage. You can't build it on lies."

13. *Logic.* This is the process of working out a conclusion from its premises. In it, you start with known facts, and combine them to gain facts that were unknown when you started.

Here is a very simple example:

"That little boy is crying. That woman over there is running frantically around, as though she had lost something. I wonder if he couldn't be lost, and she couldn't be his mother."

Or, to use a classic example:

"All men are human.

" Aristotle is a man.

"Therefore, Aristotle is human."

Logic, therefore, is *the art of linking relations in a new way.* It is therefore, intimately dependent upon Connectors. It hinges upon the Connectors *is, are,* and *therefore.*

It is also the art of arranging overlapping definitions. So that two definitions *(All men are human* and *Aristotle is a man)* produce a third *(Therefore, Aristotle is human).*

It is an extremely powerful structure of thought. And much of our civilization is indebted to it.

So there you have them. Thirteen elaboration structures to help move your thought from beginning to end. From introduction to conclusion.

There are more of them, of course. These are only a start. It would pay you to keep your own list, and add a new structure each time you encounter it.

Above all, however, all of these structures are not rules, or matrixes, or formulas at all. They are simply opportunities. They are to be chosen when you see fit to use them in your thought-flow. To be altered to fit that thought-flow. And to be discarded entirely when you do not see fit to use them.

There is no rigidity about them. You are not a machine. You are a creative human being. These rules, therefore, are only guidelines for your own powers of invention and expression.

They give you the verbal tools to work with. But you can combine and blend them as you will.

They are much the same as being shown the right way to hold a golf club, and swing. When you are first shown this new way, you will be stiff, and your swing will be unnatural.

In other words, you will be consciously following the rules. And you will therefore be swinging mechanically.

But after a while, you will get used to these new rules, and then they will fade from your mind, and become part of your reflexes. You won't memorize them, or recite them, or even think about them. They will simply by then be part of the way you do something. But this time, you will do it more effectively – and more easily.

**Exercises and Applications
for Chapter 10**

So now we have explored communication from the first words you set down on paper to the final discourse.

We have seen that words combine to form images. Then the images combine to form sentences. Then the sentences combine to form core ideas and their elaborations. And then the core ideas combine to form your final discourse.

This is the process of communication. And grammar is the tool we use to tie it all together.

What is new in this chapter is the last step of this process: *elaboration.*

For the following exercises, circle the correct choices and fill in the blanks.

As we have seen, *elaboration is the process of developing your flow of thought, from sentence to sentence.*

1.   You do this in the following way:

You choose a core idea. You tell your listener all the details she has to know about it, in as many sentences as this takes. And then you connect that c_____ onto the next core idea.

2.   So *elaboration* involves these three steps:
- Choosing your core idea.
- Choosing the way you want to elaborate it.
- And choosing the way you're going to bridge it into your next _____.

3.   Let's put this process to work a few times, and become familiar with its nuts and bolts.

Let's start with this example:

"The first movement in the standard Armed Forces morning exercises is called the Jumping Jack. Here's how you do it:

"Stand erect, with your hands at your sides, and your feet spread comfortably apart.

"Now, at the count of 1, jump. Let your feet shoot out

till they are about twenty-four inches apart. And let your hands circle out till you clap them above your head.

"Then, at the count of 2, resume the starting position. Bring your feet together again. And let your hands fall to your sides.

"At 3, jump again. At 4, resume the starting position. At 5, jump again. And so forth, until you have done 100 counts.

"You are then ready to begin the second exercise – the Deep Knee Bends ... "

Here we have the simplest elaboration structure of all – *instruction*.

The core idea here, in all these sentences and paragraphs, is how to perform the first e_____, the Jumping Jack.

4.   The introduction to this core idea is given in the first p_____.

5.   That paragraph names the exercise, and tells the reader that he is now about to learn how to _____ it.

6.   The thought-flow then shifts focus, in the next paragraph, into the first position of the exercise. Since there is a shift in focus here, we use a new pa_____.

7.   The second paragraph, therefore, shows the starting position of the exercise.

We then shift focus again, into the third _____.

8.   In this third paragraph, we show the second position of this exercise. And we tie the third paragraph into the second paragraph by beginning it with the time Connector N_____.

9.   In this third paragraph, we wish to describe the second position to our reader completely. To do this, we have to use _____ sentences in this paragraph.

10.   But since these three sentences all have the same focus – the second p_____ of the exercise – they all belong in that same paragraph.

11.   Now, however, we shift focus again. We tell our reader that, at the count of 2, he is to resume the s_____ position.

12.   So, because we have shifted focus again, we start a new _____ again.

13.   And, to tie this fourth paragraph again into our flow of thought, we start it with another time Connector, t_____.

14.   Again, we wish to describe thoroughly what happens to our reader when she resumes the starting position. So we use _____ sentences in this paragraph to do so.

So now we have described the full exercise. We have shown our reader the starting position, and the spread-apart position. And then we have brought her back to the starting position again.

15.   She now knows the full exercise. And we can shift _____ again, and use the fifth paragraph to tell her how many times we want her to do this exercise each morning.

When she has done 100 counts, she is finished with this first exercise. And we have given her our first core idea.

16.   So, in our next paragraph, we are now ready to make the transition to our second _____.

17.   This second core idea is the s_____ exercise – the Deep Knee Bends.

18.   And we use, as our bridge between these two exercises, the time Connector t_____.

19.   So we have stated a core idea. And elaborated it in five paragraphs. And used the sixth paragraph to make the transition between it and the next core idea.

We have used, as our example, the simplest elaboration-structure: In _____.

20.   But we could just as easily have used the other elaboration-structures: Narrative ... reasons-why ... causes ... effects ... description ... contrast ... examples ... explanation ... definition ... logic ... or the rest.

In all these cases, the same basic procedure would have held:

   • First, choose a core idea.

- Next, choose the way you want to elaborate on it.
- And finally, choose the way you are going to bridge it in to your next _____.

Now, in each one of these elaboration-structures, the shifts in focus will take place in different spots. And you will start new paragraphs to indicate these shifts.

For example, in narration, a standard shift in focus (and therefore new paragraph) takes place when a new character begins to speak.

Like this:

"But you can't leave me like this," she said.

"But I can," he replied.

"But what about everything you've promised me?" she whined.

"That was three lifetimes ago," he snarled back at her.

And so on. This, incidentally, is one of the reasons fiction is so loved by millions of people. Not only for its content. But because its dialogue allows for constant short shifts of focus. And thus, short p_____. And thus, easy reading.

Description can be handled the same way. Take the description of a person, for example. You can describe her entire appearance in one paragraph. Or you can use separate paragraphs for her face, her body, her clothes, etc.

The choice is up to you. As we've seen, you can make your paragraphs longer or shorter, just as you have the choice of making your sentences longer or shorter.

The same freedom of choice holds for reasons, causes, effects, examples, and documentations. We have seen excellent examples in this chapter of how they can all be broken down into small, simple paragraphs, so the reader can grasp them at once.

So let's leave my examples, and work on one of yours. Right now, why don't you choose one of the elaboration-structures, and let's work out its development from core idea to core idea.

21.   You start by choosing your first core idea. Write it in your first sentence here:

_____

_____

22.   Now name the elaboration-structure you are going to use to develop it here:

_____

_____

23.   How are you going to bridge between the introduction of your core idea and its first elaboration? Write your transition phrase or sentence here:

_____

_____

24.   Now I imagine you are ready for your first shift in focus. So write your second paragraph here:

_____

_____

_____

_____

25.   What Connector did you use in that second paragraph to tie it in with the first? (Or in the first, to signal the development of the second?) Write it here: _____.

26.   Now you shift focus again, and write your third paragraph here:

_____

_____

_____

_____

27.   Write that paragraph's Connector here:

_____

28.   And now write your fourth paragraph here:

_____

_____

_____

_____

29.   And your fourth paragraph's Connector here:

_____

30.   And now let's limit this elaboration of that first core idea to the previous four paragraphs. So you are ready to switch to a new core idea.

Write that transition sentence to that new core idea here:

_____

_____

_____

_____

And so forth. As you can immediately see, we have gone beyond mere exercises, and into actual discourse itself.

In other words, you are now professionally communicating. You are telling someone else – either by speaking or by writing – your thoughts. You are using the tools you have learned in this book to achieve your own ends. But you are going beyond the power of the book itself to help you control your effectiveness in attaining these ends.

In other words, you are on your own. You are the judge now. You have the tools. You have the ideas. You have the need to express them.

And it only remains for you to put them together. Once again, good luck – and good communicating.

PART TWO

HOW TO MAKE WHAT YOU SAY OR WRITE UNFORGETTABLE!

Chapter 11

If You're Going to Say It, Say It So It Will Be Quoted All Over Town

As YOU'VE SEEN, this book is not about *what* you think, but how you *say* what you think. Because sometimes, *how* you say something is as important as *what* you say.

Let me give you an example. Let's say that you, like most people, are dissatisfied with the way things are going in this country recently. And let's say that you want to express this feeling – in either a social conversation, or a business conference, or even a speech in front of a group of people. So you're going to put words together, to express this feeling. But *how* are you going to put those words together? Are you going to say it in a straight, bland, completely forgettable way, like this:

"I think that this country is running downhill, and things are getting worse every day."

This expresses the thought all right. But it does it in such a way that you sound like everybody else... that your audience will yawn when you say it... and they'll forget it one minute later.

So how do you do it in a way that makes this perfectly true, but rather common thought seem brand-new again? That gives it punch? That not only informs your audiences of what you think, but gives them a smile as well?

Well, you take the same basic thought, and you rephrase it

something like this:

"There has been a lot of progress during my lifetime, but I'm afraid it's headed in the wrong direction."

See the difference? Both sentences express the same thought. But the first is predictable and flat as a pancake ... while the second sentence takes you by surprise, amuses as well as informs you, and makes the thought stick. In fact, it's quotable. Other people will pick it up, remember it, and use it on their friends. And they may very well tell them that it comes from you, just as I'm now informing you that it actually comes from Ogden Nash.

Now, why would anyone want to talk in flat sentences like our first example, when she could just as easily talk, and write, in punchy sentences like our second example? And when she could fill every one of her conversations, or reports, or letters, or speeches with exactly this kind of quotable phrase – *not* copied from someone else, but manufactured by herself, to order, right on the spot.

All right. You'll agree to all this, I'm sure. Of course you'd rather express yourself like this. But how do you do it? Until now, the only people who could express themselves that memorably were writers, artists, and other natural-born "phrase-makers." And all the rest of us could do was copy them.

That was – until now!

You see, what's happened in the last few years is that we've discovered the *rules* that make these punchy statements work. These are the very rules that these "brilliant" phrase-makers used themselves, although I think they did so unconsciously.

But now these rules *have* been made conscious, and deliberate, and are quite usable by everybody. These rules are based on a few simple facts – which you've just read in the first part of this book. There, these rules are used in a straightforward direction, to help you speak clearly, so that anyone can understand what you say at once.

Here, however, we turn these same rules around, and create deliberate double meanings – so your reader still understands what you say, but now it has an extra *double* punch.

Ogden Nash did this, in our sample sentence above, by creating a deliberate double meaning for the word "progress." His double meaning in this sentence was this: As you know, "progress" usually means "getting better." And that's the way he seemed to use it in the first part of his sentence – *"There has been a lot of progress in my lifetime."*

So far, so good. It looks, up to now, like a perfectly normal statement; and we're cruising right along, effortlessly, with Mr. Nash. And then he drops the bomb on us! Then he *twists* the meaning of the word "progress" – gives it a new, double meaning by saying, *"but I'm afraid it's headed in the wrong direction."*

So "progress" all of a sudden doesn't mean "getting better," but now means "getting worse." Nash has fooled us. He's slipped in a double meaning on us. He's caught us in the middle of his sentence, forced us to come screeching to a stop, and think twice about what he's *really* saying, and then laugh our heads off at the way he's saying it.

So he is using a very simple rule in composing that sentence, that gives that sentence its punch. And that rule is this:

Set up a double meaning in the first part of the sentence, and exploit it in the second!

But this rule is a little advanced. And so it may be a little confusing to you right now. So we'll have to work up to it in stages, till you can feel as comfortable with it as Nash did.

And let's start looking at these stages now.

Chapter 12

The Basic Rule Underlying All Quotable Statements

L ET'S START WITH a fundamental definition:

An epigram is a single sentence, which, by the way it's stated, makes its content twice as strong as it would otherwise be.

This definition tells us several things. First, it tells us that an epigram (a punchy sentence) has nothing to do with *the content* that it expresses. That content can be anything whatsoever. That content does not have to be strong or dramatic or funny in itself. *It is the way you phrase that content that adds the strength, and the drama, and the wit.*

Second, this definition tells us that an epigram is a single sentence. A "one-liner," as stand-up comedians call it. This means that the epigram is necessarily short. Therefore, it is quick; its punch comes fast; it's easily remembered, and easily retold.

And, since it is short, the epigram must also necessarily be simple. Because there just isn't enough room in that single sentence for it to get complicated – not if it wants to retain its punch.

And punch it must. Because the entire essence of an epigram is the strength its phraseology gives its content.

Now, to set up any punch – physical or verbal – you need at least two ingredients. One of them sets up the punch. And the other delivers it.

For example, to deliver his punch, a boxer must first pull back his arm (part one), and then swing it forward (part two). And a golfer has her backswing, and then her delivery. And so does a tennis player, a billiards player, a squash player... or any player at all who has to deliver a great deal of concentrated energy, fast, to a fixed point.

And exactly the same rule works in the epigram. Every epigram therefore has at least two parts. One part to set up the punch. And a second part to deliver it.

So we can now expand our original definition like this:

An epigram is a single sentence, of at least two parts, which by the way they verbally work together, make the content twice as strong as it ordinarily would be.

Now, how do these two simple, short sentence parts work together to deliver their punch? This is the critical question. And the answer is equally simple:

By contrast!

Epigrams work by *contrast!*

The basic structure of every epigram is the deliberate contrast between one word and another; or between one meaning of a word, and another meaning of that same word.

Let me give you two quick examples. The first shows the power of contrasting two opposite words:

"He who praises everybody praises nobody." – Samuel Johnson

And the basic structure of this epigram lies in the contrast of the words "everybody" and "nobody." And we can diagram that basic structure like this:

everybody-nobody

And, again, we could take exactly the same thought, and almost the same phraseology, and express it much more weakly, simply by leaving out the contrast. Like this:

"He who praises everybody reduces the value of that praise to almost nothing."

Notice how flabby that second sentence seems in comparison to the first. Notice how it dwindles off into banality. Why? Because the *everybody-nobody* contrast is missing. The thought is still there, but the punch is gone.

So Johnson picks two perfectly ordinary words out of the dictionary, and puts them together in a sharp new way to make a statement that people have repeated down through the centuries.

And did he do this deliberately? Of course. In going from the original, preverbal thought to the phrasing of that thought, he sends out a search -command in his own brain something like this:

What two contrasting words express this thought most sharply?

And it's this kind of search-command that I'm trying to teach you today. I can't give you the answers – the actual word-contrasts themselves – because there are an infinite number of them to choose from. But I can give you the search-questions that produce them for you, when you need them for a particular occasion.

So what you're learning in this book are questions. Demands. Search-directions that tell your brain in what general areas to look for the right combinations. And then the brain, now that it knows where it's going, will deliver those combinations right back to you.

And the first of these search-commands – and the most important – is this:

Look for contrast!

Epigrams, once again, are built from contrast. They get their quick, sharp punch from contrast. And the first kind of contrast that they're built from is the contrast of two opposite words.

The second kind of contrast is not between two words, but between two meanings of the same word. In other words, a word whose meaning changes in mid-sentence. Like this:

"Last night, in Hamlet, Mr. S _____ played the king as though he expected someone to play the ace." – George G. Nathan.

Here, in this stinging one-sentence review, the contrast

depends on the difference between the two meanings of the word "play." The first meaning of "play," of course, is "to play a role." And the second meaning of "play" is "to play cards." And what Mr. Nathan does, to slash poor Mr. S _____ to ribbons, is simply to change the meaning of "play" in the middle of this sentence.

So we can diagram this contrast like this:

play a role-play a card

And what search-command did Mr. Nathan use here? Probably something like this:

What word's meaning can I switch to express how lousy this man's acting really is?

And his further thought process, in response to that search-question, was probably something like this:

An actor *plays* a role. That gives me the word *play,* with all its accompanying images. So can I use *play* in a different way to get the effect I want? Sure, if I switch its meaning to *play cards* ... then to *play bridge* ... and then narrow it right down to *playing the ace on someone else's king.*

Of course, all this took place unconsciously, and almost instantly, because Nathan was already an accomplished and practiced phrase-maker. But you, who are just learning how to operate these search-mechanisms, will have to go through the same process quite consciously, step by step, till you become as familiar with it as he was.

It's almost exactly like learning a tennis swing. Let's say you have a backhand now, but far too weak and too undependable a one. So you go to a pro, and then the pro shows you the right commands to give your body to build power into that backhand. They consist of a new way to grip the racket, to position yourself toward the ball, to set your arm, to hit the ball, to follow through, etc. And, at the beginning, each one of these commands has to be given, and obeyed, consciously. And, if they are so given and obeyed, then they provide the solution to that particular shot, coming to you at that particular position on the court, for individual shot after shot.

But after a while, as you grow more familiar with them, they fade out of your conscious mind, and into your unconscious. And then they work faster and better for you.

And the same thing happens here. First, you learn the search-commands. Then you practice them, step by step. And then you get them down to the point where they work automatically, by themselves, bringing you combinations that you couldn't possibly have anticipated before.

So, now you've seen two kinds of contrast – the contrast between two words of opposite meaning ... and the contrast between two opposite meanings of the same word. So let's go on now to a third kind of contrast, which is more subtle, but still as slashingly effective. And it's contained in this example:

"There is always an easy solution to every human problem – neat, plausible, and wrong." – H. L. Mencken

Now, the contrast here hinges on the conventional meaning of the word "solution," and the entirely different new meaning which Mencken gives to it by the last word of his sentence. The conventional meaning, of course, is "right answer to a problem." And Mencken's contrasting new meaning is, quite simply, "wrong answer to a problem."

So the basic structure of this razor-sharp little sentence is this:

(solution = right answer) - wrong answer

In other words, in the first half of this sentence, Mencken says *"There is always an easy solution to every human problem..."* And, when we first see these words, we interpret them to mean this: *"There is always an easy (right answer) to every human problem ..."* So, in our minds, "solution" means " right answer." But then Mencken throws his punch at us, in the second part of the sentence, like this:" – neat, plausible, and wrong!". And he demolishes us, because now "solution" is no longer equal to "right answer"; but has suddenly, in mid-sentence, become equal to "wrong answer."

Powerful? Very. Because he lets us think that he's using "solution" in the conventional way, with the conventional meaning. And then out of a clear blue sky he hits us with a contrasting meaning of that same word before we even know what's happening.

And this, of course, is exactly the same mechanism that Ogden Nash used in the quote I gave you in the previous chapter. There, as you remember, he said:

"There has been a lot of progress during my lifetime, but I'm afraid it's headed in the wrong direction."

Again, he sets us up in the first part, and socks us in the second. In the first part, he lets us think that he's using the word, "progress" as meaning "movement in the right direction". And then, in the second part, he says, "oh no! Progress just means 'movement', in any direction. And I say it's been moving just now in the wrong direction!"

So we can diagram the basic structure of this sentence something like this:

(progress = right direction) - wrong direction

So, again, contrast! But this time the contrast between the conventional, accepted meaning of a word, and the opposite meaning that the author gives it in this particular sentence.

And probably the search-command you will give yourself to produce this kind of contrast is this:

How can I take the conventional meaning of this word and flip it head-over-heels, so I can shock my audience into seeing what I see?

So now we've seen the three main kinds of contrast that go to make up our punchy little epigrams. They are, once again:

1.   Contrast between two words with opposite meanings.
2.   Contrast between two opposite meanings of the same word.
3.   Contrast between the conventional meaning of a

word, and a new, opposite meaning that the author gives that word in his epigram.

Of course, we'll see many more examples of each kind of these three contrasts in the chapters to follow. But, always, in every case, contrast forms the basic structure of the epigram. The epigram is, in fact, built on contrast. So our basic formula for composing epigrams – for speaking and writing sentences that punch – is this simple two-word formula:

Use contrast!

Look for *contrast* first. And then build the rest of your epigram around it. That's the key. And that's the first search-command you should give your brain:

Where can I use CONTRAST here?

Chapter 13

How To Create Quotable Statements, Not Only In Your Writing, But In Your Spontaneous Conversation

SO NOW WE have our main rule. And what you're going to learn from the rest of this book are simply the varying ways of applying it.

Now, what do these applications consist of? Well, they consist of a coming-together – an accidental flowing-together – of two very dissimilar things:

the events that happen to you every day; and

the inventory of words and phrases and meanings that you carry around with you in your brain.

You see, the things that happen to you every day – the problems, the meetings, the conversations, the telephone calls, the interchanges of any kind between you and other people – all these individual events are really the opportunities life gives you to create your own epigrams. And the inventory of words and meanings in your head are the raw materials out of which you then shape these epigrams, so that they fit precisely the individual event that you need one of them for at that moment.

Of course, there are literally thousands upon thousands of different events that you participate in during your lifetime. And there are also thousands upon thousands of different words and phrases stored up in your memory. So no one could possibly give you a "Dictionary of Ready-Made Epigrams" for use in all these infinite situations.

So you have to create your own – instantly, on the spot, and with the precision of a champion marksman, right to the center of the target.

So, therefore, you have to be taught – not repetition – but creativity. And that means, in turn, that instead of being taught answers, you have to be taught questions. Or, in another phraseology, that instead of being taught formulas, you have to be taught search-commands.

You see, if creativity can be taught at all – and I believe it can – then it can only be taught as a series of directions. Places to look. Areas to be scanned. So that what the mind does, when it receives one of these commands, is go into that memory-area ... flip through its contents, unconsciously, as fast as it can ... and see if the right answer is buried somewhere there.

If the answer is there – and that answer is always a new combination of old elements that were just sitting there before – then the mind automatically brings up that answer to the surface of consciousness. But, if the right answer isn't there – if the combination asked for just doesn't work – then you give your mind a command to search another area (either a different area or a more specific area), and it gives you another chance.

The whole process is like a woman looking for a lost child. She doesn't know, of course, where that child is. But she knows the best way to find it. She gets some friends, and they all pick one specific area where they think that child may be. Then they scan it, go through the entire area, side by side, step by step. And, if the child isn't there, they then go on to the next area ... and the next ... and the next, till they find her.

So the brain, when it's used the right way, is essentially a scanning mechanism. It sits there, waiting for commands to produce newness. *But you have to give it the right commands.* And that's what I'm trying to teach you here.

These search-commands are especially important to you when you come up against that most demanding of all epigram-situations – the instant retort. The spontaneous, on-the-spot one-liner that parries an opponent's thrust, or cuts him to pieces, and breaks up the crowd with laughter around both of you.

Here, if ever, memory is of no help whatsoever. Because you can't tell, until the instant he says it, what the content of his statement is going to be. And you can't predict, until the instant you say it, how you're going to use that statement of his as the first part of the epigram you're then going to construct to rock him.

In other words, he pitches you a word; and you use the search-command as a bat to knock it right out of the park.

And that search-command is always, basically, as simple as this:

Use contrast!

And the contrast pulls the right answer out of your brain for you (theoretically, at least) right on the spot. Like this:

W. C. Fields was a notorious child-hater. One day, while relaxing at the side of his pool, he was asked by a newspaper reporter, *"Mr. Fields, do you like any children?"*

Immediately, Fields's mind thought: *Contrast.* It seized on the word "like" in the question. And it produced the following almost-immediate reply:

"Yes, young ones. Parboiled."

Whammy! Right on target! All from taking the conventional meaning of the word "like" – which is "to like people" – and reversing it so that it suddenly comes out, "to like food."

The question was spontaneous. It couldn't have been predicted. Therefore, the answer could never have been prepared in advance. *But the search-command was prepared in advance.* And it produced the right contrast – and the right phraseology for that contrast (which we'll discuss in a minute) almost before the question had died on the reporter's lips.

Or take the two members of English Parliament in the eighteenth century. They were always quarreling, but never quite dueling, except with words. Among the most telling of these verbal duels was the day, on the floor of Parliament, when one of them, in an unaccustomed fit of modesty, said to the other:

"I, sir, am my own worst enemy."

To which the other man immediately replied:

"Not, sir, as long as I am alive."

Here, again, an unpredictable statement. Taken by the second man, and processed according to the basic command, "Use contrast." So that the word "my (own worst enemy)," in the first man's statement is immediately contrasted with the word "I (am your worst enemy)," in the second man's statement. And a direct hit is again scored.

Or take the similar example of Oscar Wilde and James McNeil Whistler, in the London of the 1870s. Both were famed wits. Both were continually striving to outdo the other in verbal blockbusters. And, one night, when Wilde had made a particularly telling remark, Whistler said:

"By George, Oscar, I wish I'd said that."

To which Mr. Wilde immediately replied:

"You will, James. You will."

And what is the contrast structure here? It is the grasping of the words, *"had said that"* in the first statement, and the immediate contrast to them of the words *"you will (say that)"* in the second statement.

Or, as one final example, let us look at Gertrude Stein – a compulsive phrase-maker, even under the most inappropriate circumstances. Even at the very moment of her death, she managed to top her own statement, in the following way.

As she lay dying, Miss Stein turned to her lifelong friend, Alice B. Toklas, and in a hoarse whisper asked:

"Alice, what is the answer?"

And Miss Toklas replied:

"I don't know."

Whereupon Miss Stein then said, a brief moment before she died:

"Then what is the question?"

Here, the contrast is clear: *Answer - question.* A search-and-produce mechanism so thoroughly ingrained in this remarkable woman's life that it operated even as the brain that sustained it faded from the light.

So the secret of spontaneity – in this as in all the other examples – is search-command. Direction. Where to look. And the first of these directions is: *Contrast.*

And now let us go on to examine some of the others.

Chapter 14

Implication: The Key To Making Your Audience Furnish the Final Punch to What You Say or Write

N OW WE TURN for a moment from the basic structure of the epigram – which is always hidden beneath the surface – to the surface itself.

The basic structure, as you know, is *contrast*. But this contrast always appears *below the surface of the epigram*. It is never stated completely in the words of the epigram. *Part of it always remains unstated (in other words, implied) so that your audience can discover it themselves.*

Let's go back to our previous examples, and see how this works.

Take the W. C. Fields example. As you remember, the reporter asked Mr. Fields:

"Do you like any children?"

And Fields processed that remark, using contrast, to reverse the meaning of the word "like" from "like people" to "like food." So far, so good – as the essential first step.

But only as the first step. For now the contrast has to be recorded back up again, into words. And there are several different sets of words that Fields could have used to recode it.

For example, Fields could have simply stated the basic contrast right out in the open. And it would have come out this way:

"Yes, I like them – not as people – but as food."

Fine. The contrast is still there. But the punch is gone. Why? For two reasons: First, because the phrase "not as people" tips the audience off that the twist is to take place – that an opposite meaning is about to be used – and therefore robs the rest of the sentence of its surprise. It's much like a boxer telegraphing his punch. If he does, it never lands.

Secondly, this dragging of the structure to the surface also makes the thought too crude and too complete to be really effective. It makes it too crude because even Mr. Fields doesn't *really* want to eat children; he just wants to use that image to shock his audience a little. And it makes it too complete because it gives the audience nothing to do. It hands them the *finished* image too soon and too bluntly, and they just won't accept it that way.

Therefore, instead of stating the final image (that he is going to redefine children as food) in so many words, good old W. C. very shrewdly substituted *the next-to-final-image* as the content for his actual wording.

In other words, he let his audience *discover for them-selves* the final, underlying image, *by working out in their heads the implications of the one-step-removed words he actually used.*

So his final wording was this:

"Yes. Young ones. Parboiled."

And, again, in that final phraseology, there is no mention of the words "food" or "eat." Because these are final images, and they should never therefore be stated by the actor (yourself, from now on), but only discovered by the audience.

And so the full process of constructing the epigram goes like this. A starting word or image (in this case, "like") is either given to you by your audience (in this case, the reporter), or chosen by yourself.

That starting image then disappears out of sight. It is sent by your search-command into the unconscious, where a contrast is selected to give you the raw material for your reply.

The contrast, however, is still just a thought – actually bare relationship between the starting image you were given, and the final image you wish to end up with. *But that final image should end up in your audience's mind.* So you need an in between stage – your actual words themselves, which will be one-step-removed from that final image, but that will lead your audience inevitably right into it.

So Fields was given the word "like." And he sent down a search-command to come up with the basic contrast of twisting its meaning from "like people" to "like food." And then he sent out a search-command something like this:

What word, one-step-removed from "food", will force that person to realize that I've twisted his "like-children-as-people" into "like-children-as-food"?

And he came up immediately (and still subconsciously) with this answer:

Parboiled, of course! Because that is a particular way we prepare food!

So he now had the final step to close the chain between starting image and final image. When he said, "parboiled," the reporter had to think: "But parboiled is a way to prepare *food*. Therefore, Fields only likes any children as *food*. And as nothing else!"

All this reasoning in the audience's mind, of course, is equally unconscious. What I am doing here is tediously stretching out very rapid unconscious processes, so we can see in detail how they work. Actually they take place in split seconds – probably as fast, or faster, than the speed at which a computer works.

So there you have one complete description of the epigram process. It's best to show this complete process in conversation – in the spontaneous retort – because in this situation you see most clearly the fact that *the final step must end up in the audience's mind, not in your own words.*

So, in essence, in an epigram you have: *Contrast expressed by implication!*

And both brought simultaneously to the surface of your mind by a two-step series of search-commands. First you get your contrast. And then you get your one-step-removed implication to express it in.

Now, for one moment, let's look at some more examples of the second step of this process – the implication-command. Let's go on to our two antagonists in the English Parliament, and look at the process that was put into motion when one of them said to the other:

"I, sir, am my own worst enemy."

The contrast here, as we have seen before, lies in the transition from "I am my own worst enemy," said on the part of the first speaker, to "I am your worst enemy," implied by the words of the second speaker.

So contrast has been secured. But *implication* must still be added. And how was this done?

Well, first of all, quite obviously, *not by using the actual word* "enemy," because "enemy" is the final image, and therefore must end up in the audience's mind. And therefore it is taboo in the speaker's words.

What has to be included in the speaker's words, therefore, is the one-step-removed thought that will lead the other man to the final "enemy" image. And that one-step-removed thought will be pulled out of the unconscious by a search-command something like this:

What phrase, one step removed from the final image, will force that man to realize that he cannot be his own worst enemy as long as I am around?

This is, in other words, a contradiction of the other man's opening statement. This contradiction, if it were bluntly stated in words, would go something like this, *"You are not your own worst enemy; I am your worst enemy."*

And since the implication that expresses this contradiction must be one step removed from that final blunt
statement, it must then express *the conditions* for my
existence as an enemy. Like this:

"Not, sir, as long as I am alive."

And the full structure of the reply – both stated and
unstated – is this: *"As long as I am still alive (I am your
worst enemy)."*

I have put the unstated part of this total structure in
parentheses, to mark it off from the stated part. The stated
part, once again, appears in the speaker's words. The
unstated part appears in the audience's mind.

This is shown quite clearly in our next example – that
between Oscar Wilde and James Whistler. Here Whistler
said:

"By George, Oscar, I wish I'd said that."

And Wilde instantly took "had said" and transformed it
in his mind into its opposite, "will say," and then gained his
one-step-removed implication by simply dropping the final
image, "say" out of his reply. Like this:

"You will, James. You will."

And the total structure of this reply is simply:

"You will (say it)."

So now we see that every epigram has three parts: The
setting-up-the-punch part ... the throwing-the-punch part ...
and the landing-the-punch part. You can set up the punch
yourself, or you can let the other person unwittingly set it
up for you. You then throw the punch, by implication. And
you let the other person stick her jaw right into it, when
she figures out (instantly and unconsciously) what that
next-to-final implication leads right into.

Chapter 15

Tools that Let You Build Implication into Your Key Sentences

Hᴇʀᴇ ᴀʀᴇ ᴀ ᴅᴏᴢᴇɴ devices that let you use these lead-in structures ... and one-step-removed structures to give you the punch you want.

And how do you build in implication? By using lead-in structures – one-step-removed structures to give you your final wording. And let's look at some of them right now:

1.   *Drop off the final image, and let him fill it in for you.*

We saw one example of this implication technique in the Oscar Wilde example above. Here's another one:

> *"Ours is the age that is proud of machines that think,*
> *and suspicious of men who try to."*
> – H. Mumford Jones

Here, Mr. Jones got his contrast by opposing machines-that-think with men-that-think, and also by opposing our pride in the first to our suspicion of the second. He then got his implication by the simple device of dropping off the word "think" from the end of his sentence, so it would have to be filled in by his reader.

And the total structure of the last part of this sentence is this *"... and suspicious of men who try to (think)."*

2.   *Use a Summary Word to force the other person to redefine your first sentence-part's real meaning.*

A Summary Word is a word such *as ... it ... this ... that ... these ...* and so on, that summarizes a whole phrase used earlier in the same sentence, or the sentence that came before. Summary Words are explained in Part One of this book. There, you saw that they have several uses in carrying your main line of thought from one sentence to the next. Here, however, we are using them as an implication device, to force your audience's mind to arrive at the final image from the one-step-removed phraseology you have given them.

Here is an excellent example of this device in action:

> *"When I was a boy,*
> *I was told anybody could become president;*
> *now I'm beginning to believe it."*
> – C. Darrow

Here, Darrow uses the word "anybody" as the pivot of his epigram. His contrast-structure is based on the change in meaning of "anybody" from positive to negative ... from promise to despair. And he builds his implication at the end of the sentence by summarizing the first half-phrase, "anybody could become president," in the single word "it."

This forces the audience's mind to unconsciously stop at the word "it" ... play back the full phrase that "it" summarizes ... and, in so playing back, to realize that Darrow is now using "anybody" to mean "any old dope" rather than (as we first assumed) "any person of great promise."

And so the total structure of the last part of this sentence is this: *"... now I'm beginning to believe it (that any old dope can become president)."*

Another beautiful example of this use of summary words to gain implication is the following little gem:

> *"Of two evils, choose neither."*
> – C. Spurgeon

Notice that this five-word blockbuster uses both implication devices we have detailed so far. It uses the summary word "neither" to condense the earlier phrase, "two evils." And it uses the chop-off device by dropping off the final-image-word, "evil" from its end. So the total structure of this sentence is actually this:

> *"Of two evils, choose neither (evil)."*

3.   *Give an outward symptom, to force your audience to arrive at the inward disease.*
For example:

> *"Life is like an onion; you peel off one layer at a time,*
> *and sometimes you weep."*
> – C. Sandburg

Here we have a three-part sentence, with the contrast occurring between the second and third parts, i.e., the implied sadness appears as a surprise only in the last word. And it appears, not by Sandburg saying that life is "sad" but by his giving us the prime symptom by which we know someone else is sad – weeping.
So the total structure of the last part of that sentence is this: *"... and sometimes you weep (because it is so sad)."*
4.   *Switch the meaning of two words in your epigram, so that their meanings at the end are different than they were at the beginning.*
For example:

> *The two most engaging powers of the author are to*
> *make new things familiar, and familiar things new."*
> – William Thackery

What you do here is reverse the position of the two key words as the sentence proceeds. By doing this, each gives the other new meaning.
Admittedly, this mechanism lacks a bit of the punch that the others had. It is therefore more quietly absorbed by

your reader. What he feels, as he passes a sentence like this, is – not shock, per se – but strength. Almost no time is needed here to feed back. A stronger point in the sentence is made – but gently.

Here are some other examples:

> *"We have modified our environment so radically that to exist in this new environment we must now modify ourselves."*
> – Norbert Weiner

> *"As machines get to be more and more like men, men will become more like machines."*
> – J. Crutch.

> *"There is great ability in knowing how to conceal ability."*
> – F. La Rochefoucauld

As you see, in the last example the change in meaning of only a single word forces your reader to think more deeply.

5.   *The super twist. Where you take your reader on a real mind trip, through your unexpected end-definition.*

For example:

> *"Bureaucracy defends the status quo long past the time when the quo has lost its status."*
> – L. Peter

This statement derives its power from the break-up of a cliche. So we think of it for a moment, *status quo* means that the quo is still "statusing." But it really may not be "statusing" at all any longer. This statement, phrased as it is, wakes us up violently to that fact.

> *"Computers are fantastic: in a few minutes they can make a mistake so great that it would take many men many months to equal it."*
> – M. Meacham

Again, the second part of the sentence not only contradicts the first, but also contradicts the common belief of the readers as well. It hits you square in your assumptions. Therefore it stings, it shocks, it awakes.

> *"Traditionalists are pessimistic about the future*
> *and optimists about the past."*
> – L. Mumford

Again, in this surprising last twist of phrasing, we find the shock of truth.

> *"He who trims himself to suit everybody*
> *will soon whittle himself away."*
> – R. Hull

This is used here as a metaphor, of course. But we don't expect the author to extend that metaphor quite so far. When he does, therefore, it takes a surprising little bite out of our expectations.

> *"Unhappiness is not knowing what we want,*
> *and killing ourselves to get it."*
> – D. Herold

Who would kill ourselves to get something that we don't even know we want? All of us – that's who!

> *"Ideas won't keep:*
> *something must be done about them."*
> – A. N. Whitehead

This is strictly metaphor. Ideas here are compared to fruit. If nothing is done about them, they spoil. No word-twists are involved, but the sting is there, in all its sharpness and indelibility.

6. *The surprise definition. Redefining a word in the phrase so you take your reader, or your listener, completely off guard.*
For example:

> *"My way of joking is to tell the truth.*
> *It's the funniest joke in the world."*
> – G. B. Shaw

We don't think of the truth as a joke. Shaw does. His insistence upon its being so startles us, then amuses us, then rocks us. Even in spur-of-the-moment conversation.

> *"The slave has but one master, the ambitious man has as many masters as there are persons whose aid may contribute to the advancement of his fortune."*
> – J. de la Bruyere

Any word (here, "master") can be redefined. But redefine it with this kind of zing, and your friends will never forget it.

> *"Make three correct guesses consecutively, and you will establish a reputation as an expert."*
> – L. Peter

The surprise is contained in the last word. Once it is uttered, the listener must go back and review the entire sentence, from the beginning, to gain the full explanation of the definition – and recover from its shock. This is much more powerful than phrasing it like this:
"An expert is a fellow who ..."
Or, as another example of this technique:

> *"The average Ph.D. thesis is nothing but a transference of bones from one graveyard to another."*
> – J. Frank Dobie

This follows the standard structure of a definition – the word to be defined is given first, then its meaning. But the twisted meaning is so startling here, and so funny, that it catches us completely by surprise.

This is, of course, definition-by-metaphor. It is not a conceptual definition but a visual definition. Try this visual-definition technique yourself, wherever possible. It will produce surprisingly good results.

"Great blunders are often made,
like large ropes, of a multitude of fibers."
– V. Hugo

Another visual definition. Much stronger than any conceptual terms it might have otherwise been phrased in. Remember, the eyes of your listener's mind remember far longer than her brain.

"Thoughts are but dreams til their effects be tried."
– W. Shakespeare

This is a time definition: X is Y till its effects, over a period of time, are known. It is especially good for scientific papers, reports, management appraisals, stock forecasts. Store this time definition in your mind. It will prove to be a handy tool, over and over again.

Once again, let's analyze how you gain this metaphorical power. A metaphor is an equation. It equates the idea contained in one word to the idea contained in another word. It simply assumes that they are the same.

For example, the idea or image in "ship" is compared in a metaphor to the idea or image contained in "plow." By such a comparison, you get to use all the new images of the plow to describe the ship more vividly.

Much of the time, in serious writing, you're dealing with ideas instead of images. Ideas contain a lot of conceptual and intellectual power, but have almost no emotional or memorable power.

For example, "hypothesis" has zero emotional power. But "bones in a graveyard" hits you right in the gut – or, in this case, in the funnybone.

Also, metaphors not only contain images, but models. A model is an image that you can see developing in a certain set pattern over time. Take "ropes and fibers." You not only see the rope and its fibers, but you go on to see the individual fibers winding around each other, and pulling together to gain the united strength of the massive rope they then form.

That pattern – that joining together from fragile to unbreakable – is all available in the "fiber-rope" image. But when you use it in comparison to the "blunder" idea, you then see that blunders also go from fragility at the beginning, to unbreakability at the end. And you see it in a way that moves you to do something about them ... and also sticks in your memory from then on.

Why not, then, weld emotional power onto intellectual power, through metaphor? Again, you do this by switching languages – from abstract thoughts to eye-filling images – all in the same sentence.

Start those sentences abstractly ... then switch in their middle into visual. Borrow all the images, all the models, all the surprises that such a switch gives you.

> *"A baby is God's opinion*
> *that the world should go on."*
> – C. Sandburg

This epigram – another time definition – reaches to the height of poetry. The sublime, as you see, is constructed on exactly the same rules as the merely amusing.

What is the search-command that pulls this kind of twist out of your memory? *What doesn't go here?* Children are not to be eaten. Indecision is not habitual. Status never loses its quo. You never want to conceal your ability. Etc.

All these comparison-pairs are joined by "nots" or "nevers." Those "nots" or "nevers" are like a brick sitting on a spring. Take it off, and you get an explosive release of energy.

Look for the not. Look for the never. Look for the impolite. Look for the shocking. Look for any rule that says, "You mustn't go here." For that's where the real punch lies.

7.   *The last-word contradiction. Where the last word of the epigram contradicts all that has gone before it.*

For example:

> *"There is always an easy solution*
> *to every human problem*
> *– neat, plausible, and wrong."*
> – H. Mencken

Here, the truth does not emerge till the final word. We are led in one direction, and then shown that it tumbles us right off the edge of a cliff. Very powerful. A little sneaky. But so is the world it maps.

> *"Bride: A woman with a fine prospect of*
> *happiness behind her."*
> – A. Bierce

This contradiction is perfectly logical, and totally unexpected. The reader, therefore, can have no complaint. He was fooled here by nothing more than his own preconceptions.

Every time you learn of such preconceptions in your audience, you have a tool to trick them, educate them, shock them, amuse them in a way that would not be possible without such preconceptions.

> *"The first and worst of all frauds is to cheat oneself.*
> *All sin is easy after that."*
> – J. Bailey

A slight modification of this category. The word "sin" does not quite come at the end of the epigram. What it does come after – the first sentence – is easily accepted, and thus sets up the punch of all that is to follow. This statement might therefore have been more powerful if the second sentence were restructured:

"After that, all sin is easy."

Here are some others:

> *"Golden shackles are far worse than iron ones."*
> – M. Gandhi

*"There is no more miserable human being than one in
whom nothing is habitual but indecision."*
– W. James

A more erudite, and therefore softer, use of this structure. It is especially useful when sprinkled throughout a long paper, to relieve the weight of fact contained in it. It obtains a wry smile as the reader follows you along, through page after page of intense logic.

*"I am free of all prejudice.
I hate everyone equally."*
– W. C. Fields

The statement is perfectly true. But it hits us over the head like a hammer, using our preconceptions to beat us into the ground.

*"Now is the time for all good men
to come to the aid of themselves."*
– F. Nelson

This is the restating of a common statement to express its opposite thought. All is fine, as we have seen before, until the closing word.

Incidentally, are you beginning to see the immense, power of these techniques, in these repeated examples?

*"In matters of conscience,
the law of the majority has no place."*
– M. Gandhi

Here we see the use of these structures to raise expression to the level of the profound, as well as the merely shocking and amusing. Gandhi is stating a desperately important truth. But with the placement of the full meaning at its very end of the sentence, he makes sure that there is no way the reader can possibly forget it again.

"There is only one giant machine operated by pygmies,
and that is bureaucracy."
– H. de Balzac

Again, only after the reader has read the full sentence, can she understand its full meaning. Thus she must review the entire epigram again, to get its full impact.

"We're about to enter the age of flight,
before we've even developed a chair
that a man can sit on comfortably."
– P. Wylie

Again, the contrast between the super-technical word *flight,* and the old-fashioned word *chair.* Much stronger than if you merely stated the contrast abstractly.

"All that is necessary for the triumph of evil
is that good men do nothing."
– E. Burke

The ultimate metaphorical contest – between *evil* and *good.* Here put by Burke to a fresh use.

"Happiness is not a station you arrive at,
but a manner of traveling."
– M. Runbek

Look for a contrasting set of images that convey your theme to your listener through his eye, instead of through his intellect. It will be ten times as striking as if you stated it the ordinary way.

"The trouble with our age is it's all sign posts
and no destinations."
– L. Kronenberger

All he's saying is that we have so much information now, that we don't know what to do with it. But he says it so, so much better than that. Because he's speaking to our eyes, and not only to our mind.

Here are a few more:

> *"A pat on the back is only a few vertebrae removed*
> *from a kick in the pants,*
> *but is miles ahead in results."*
> – V. Wilcox

> *"Next to knowing when to seize an opportunity,*
> *the most important thing in life is*
> *to know when to forgo an advantage."*
> – B. Disraeli

> *"Men build too many walls,*
> *and not enough bridges."*
> – Y. Pire

8.   *The pun. Used to heighten the kick even more.*

I don't particularly like this style myself, so I will give you just one example of it, and then pass on. Here it is:

> *"Man has made his bedlam; let him lie in it."*
> – F. Allen

Use it as you see fit. But, please, always with caution.

9.   *A surprising use of opposites.*

For example:

> *"The girl who's easy to get may be hard to take."*
> – F. Wisely

Easy – hard. East to get – hard to take. It seems pretty obvious now, doesn't it? You've come a long way since we've first started.

Here are some more examples:

> *"An expert is one who knows more and more*
> *about less and less."*
> – N. Butler

This is a fairly famous line now. It almost looks as if you could have done it yourself, with all the techniques you now have at your fingertips. Right?

> *"Very simple ideas lie within the reach*
> *only of complex minds."*
> – R. de Gourmonte

The mechanism here sticks right out and strikes you in the eye now. You're becoming sensitized to the structure of epigrams. Soon you'll be able to pick them out of your own emerging thoughts equally as easily.

> *"Success has made beggars of many men."*
> – C. Adams

What a beautiful way to say it. Could you pack as much punch into a few words?

> *"You see things, and you say 'Why?'*
> *But I see things that never were and I say 'Why not?'"*
> – G. B. Shaw

One of the great sayings of all time. And look how simply constructed it is, once you know the rules.

10. *Humorous repetition – varied with a slight change of meaning.*

For example:

> *"A committee is a group of the unprepared,*
> *appointed by the unwilling,*
> *to do the unnecessary."*
> – F. Allen

Just look at the three words – *unprepared, unwilling, unnecessary.* All of them begin with *un* – stringing them together gives you the punch. And there are so many sets of exactly such words. Such as these:

"When everyone is someone, then no one's anyone."
– W. Gilbert

"Lo! Men have become tools of their tools."
– H. Thoreau

Exact repetition here. But the different meanings of the same word *tools* and their interplay pack a tremendous punch.

"If 50 million people say a foolish thing,
it is still a foolish thing."
– B. Russell

Here, Russell uses the same two-word phrase twice. But in the second rendition, he verifies that it always means the same thing. Great impact. Derived solely from confirming the original meaning – no matter how many people try to deny it.

"The person who uses
a lot of big words is not trying to inform you;
he's trying to impress you."
– O. Miller

Very, very true.

"It is more important to do the right thing
than to do things right."
– P. Drucker

See the difference, just shifting the order of two words can make? Take advantage of this difference any time you can.

11.   *The bounce back. When the second half of the epigram reflects the first.*

For example:

> *"If you respect your job's importance,*
> *it will return the favor."*
> – L. D. Turner

"Return the favor" does all the work here. Remember, the conclusion of the thought, the real punch line, must be implied. It must work itself out in your reader's mind. You don't have to state it, you simply set up the word flow so that he *has* to think it out by sheer logic.

> *"A man has to live with himself, and he should see to*
> *it that he always has good company."*
> – C. E. Hughes

Remember, the punch from this kind of structure is gained through redefinition at the end of the sentence. You state it a new and fresh way, and the reader discovers it automatically.

> *"We shape our buildings; thereafter they shape us."*
> – W. Churchill

Very close to the repetition device used in 10 above. Shows you how more than one of these structures can be blended together to give you even more punch per word. The variations are endless.

And, finally, as merely a summary category:

12.   *Outright word contrast.*

For example:

> *"Take care of the means,*
> *and the end will take care of itself."*
> – M. Gandhi

Here, *take care* is repeated twice. The punch is derived from the shift from *means* to *end.*

This is what you have been working on all through this book.

Now go out and use it as well as these people:

*"Those who make peaceful revolution impossible will
make violent revolution inevitable."*
– J. F. Kennedy

See the power of the combination of *peaceful revolution
impossible,* with *violent revolution inevitable.* Here is a team
of repetition and slight variation that simply cannot be
beaten in making a striking and unforgettable statement.

*"Half our mistakes in life arise from feeling where we
ought to think, and thinking where we ought to feel."*
– J. Collins

*"All the beautiful sentiments in the world
weigh less than a single lovely action."*
– J. Lowell

*"Strengthen me by sympathizing with my strengths,
not my weaknesses."*
– B. Alcott

Again *surprise.* Again, *contrast.* Again, *implication.* These
are the three fundamental rules of power-packed epigrams.
They shock your listener. They grab and hold her attention.
They keep your words echoing in her mind. She is almost
impelled to repeat them when *she* wants to be as clever as
you.

Chapter 16

Other Sentence Strengtheners

THESE TOOLS DON'T help you build implication into your sentences, but they do give any sentence more power – whether it's Information or Impact.

1.   *Scan for boredom.* Don't tell your reader more than he wants to hear at that moment. Don't drift away from your main topic. Don't weigh down his mind, and his patience, with words that block his image-creating, rather than make it effortless for him.

Pull out and throwaway. Or pull out and put in later, when they're the focus of interest.

2.   *Echo words.* These are words that repeat the same first letters, such as *"Spread sunshine, not shadow."* Three of these words begin with *s,* and there are two *sh's* also included within them.

The technical term for such echo wording is alliteration. It is a cousin to rhyming, and can be thought of as first-sound rhyming, rather than last-sound rhyming. But rhyming is too intrusive to use in prose – it calls too much attention to itself – and alliteration doesn't.

These echo words give you two benefits. They please your reader's inner ear. And they strengthen, through their echoes, what you have to say.

Remember, your reader not only sees, but hears, what she reads of yours. This is the way she first learned to read, and she unconsciously continues it her whole life.

Using alliteration, therefore, makes your writing melodic. The trick of doing this is simple. When you begin moving in your head from your image to your sentence, say the words before you write them.

Taste the sound of them as they come out. Remember, you have several words available for each picture you want to convey. Give your mind two search commands for the way you'll string them together.

First, *get the sharpest image.* Second, *get the strongest echo.* Since you have such a deep pool of words available, the precise word that will fill both commands – vision and sound – will come to you far more often than you would expect.

Build sentences of *r's.* Build sentences of *s's.* Build sentences of *d's.* Turn your writing into a symphony.

One caution, however. Alliteration works, where rhyming doesn't, because alliteration isn't noticed. So don't pile it on so much that your reader looks only at the first letter of each word in your sentence. Write nothing that has the same structure as *Peter Piper picked a peck of pickled peppers.*

What's the cure? Put one or two nonalliterative words in between each alliterative word. Keep it subtle.

3. *Parallel Phrases.* Here's an example:

"*I kissed her. She slapped me.*"

This is much sharper than "*Suddenly I kissed her. At first she was simply startled. Then she pulled back her arm and slapped me.*"

Why? Because, again, there's an echo effect. But this time you're echoing – not sound – but structure. Each sentence is three words. Each has actor ... action ... acted-upon. The actions are parallel, and one causes the other (kissed-slapped). The action goes out from the narrator in the first sentence, and comes back to him in the second.

Nothing intervenes. There's just action following action. Nothing dilutes the immediacy of that action-reaction. Because of this, much nonforced implication emerges. She doesn't think – she acts. She doesn't have to make up her mind – she knows it. Therefore, much more is said in this briefer sentence than in the second one.

Structure conveys information. You can often say as much by the implication-gaps between words as by their built-in meanings. The most beautiful example of this is the Bible. See how little narrative is used to convey vast amounts of meaning. Notice each type of parallel phrase that allows this to happen.

4.   *Split-apart synonyms. Solution* is usually thought to mean *the right answer to a problem*. But in the example about solutions, we saw that it can be profitably redefined as *the wrong answer to a problem.*

In our everyday use of language, synonyms are invaluable, because they allow you to express the same image, over and over again, in different words. This anticipates, and eliminates, monotony. It gives you a chance to resubmit the same image in different words, so that if one of them doesn't form the correct image in your reader's mind, another may.

Synonyms often work together, building an image net around an idea, synonym after synonym, until your reader has as good a grasp of that image as you do.

People often don't understand something the first time they're told it, even if it's not difficult for them. Their preconceptions may block its new meaning the first time. Or special circumstances in their particular past may obscure it that first time.

That is why you repeat at least your main points, over and over again in your elaboration. And you keep searching for synonyms, and parallel phrases, to slip in that meaning until they see its newness, and understand it.

But, as you've seen, every tool that works the right way should also be examined to see if it doesn't work the opposite way. Because *the opposite way,* in this case, doesn't mean *the wrong way.* It just means *an opposite way that's also a right way.*

So when you use synonyms, not to convey the same idea, but opposite ideas, that rupture in meaning gives you tremendous power. Why? Because first it stops your reader in her tracks. She thought she knew that two words had the same meaning, but now she suddenly finds that they don't. She has to pause and redefine.

This pause is accompanied by the shock of not being sure. You have injected her with confusion. And confusion is the womb of wisdom.

Second, of course, to escape this confusion, she has to feed back, and find out why the old shared meaning no longer works. She is now doing more than simply understanding; she is also taking apart the old and putting it back together in the new.

She is growing. She is going beyond. She is dealing with a broken conceptual universe that has its own repair built into it.

The trick here is simple. Take your idea. See if it can be phrased in two pulled-apart synonyms. If it can, place the second as the last word in your sentence, or discourse-unit. Try it out on a few people. See if they can feedback the new meaning in place of the old.

If they can, you've got what you want.

5.   *Metaphor – the use of one universe of action to see more deeply into another.* Metaphor is based on the idea that *this* can be *that.* That one word works like another. That a ship cuts through things like a plow cuts through things; therefore, *plow* can be used as a metaphor for *ship,* and you can say, *"The ship plowed through the towering waves,"* and have your reader see more deeply what you're expressing.

There are many types of metaphor – action, appearance, feeling, etc. This means that one word acts the same as another, or looks the same as another, or feels the same as another.

However, metaphor doesn't say that one is *like* the other. If the metaphor is new to your reader, it's weaker to say *the ship went through the water like a plow,* than to say, *the ship plowed through the water.* That's because the *like* tips him off that the comparison is coming. By doing this, you've cut out the surprise and freshness of that comparison.

Instead, in metaphor, you can put the second word of the comparison right up against the first word, with no *like* in between. This gives a semipoetic quality to your writing, because poetry, as one of its functions, discovers new verbal similarities in the world.

This chapter has purposely been written with more metaphor in it than the previous ones. Go over it again, this time looking for the metaphors. See how they deepen, clarify, add more punch.

6.   *Vocabulary shift.* English, like any other language, has several sub-languages built into it. There's sense language. And thought language. And trade language. And more.

This sentence combines thought language and sense language:

"Evolution has a cruel way of dealing with its failed mechanisms. It eats them."

Why have these two sentences so much power? First, because of the vocabulary shift between them. In the first sentence, you're dealing with thought words – *evolution, mechanisms.* These express more or less complicated ideas. Your reader therefore understands them with his mind, rather than sees them with his eyes, or feels them with his guts.

But in the second sentence, your vocabulary shifts to sense language. It no longer maintains the thought vocabulary, like *disposes of them,* to make its point. It no longer allows you to use your mind to absorb the sentence. Instead, it abruptly, without warning, throws you into a visual image. A threatening image. A painful image.

Second, the abrupt shift is *unexpected* – therefore even

more powerful. And third, it's short and monosyllabic. You absorb it instantly – reading the three words as one – so it cuts into you like a knife.

You think with one set of words. Make love with another. Lend other people your eyes with another. Each of these sets of words is a separate channel of communication available to you. Your mind, your senses, your feelings. Blend them together, as your body does constantly, and they reinforce one another's power.

Where can these vocabulary shifts occur in your writing? Between sentences, yes. But also, of course, within sentences. For example, in a sentence above, I said *you absorb it instantly – reading the three words as one.*

Here, using the dashes as a bridge, I shifted from thought language to vision language. This allowed me to state the same image in two different ways – to reinforce it in those readers who understand it the first time, and to repeat it in different words for those who did not.

See your reader as a TV set. Each sub-language she knows is a different channel open to you. Send her multiple messages on all these channels, so that, anywhere she tunes in, you'll reach her.

7.   *Once a metaphor shift has been established, follow it as long as it adds power.* See the paragraph above. Three sentences, incorporating three metaphor elaborations: *TV set – channel – tunes in.*

Remember, once you bring in a new metaphor, you bring in a new universe. Each metaphor is not only part of a sub-language, but also part of the specialized group of words that talk about that universe.

If you say *Jesus,* for example, the entire universe of Christianity opens up to you. You can then go on to use *cross, resurrection, speaking in tongues, Judgment Day,* etc.

If you say *fumble,* then the universe of football opens up for you. You can go on to use *pass, end run, instant playback, side lines,* etc.

But beware: *A metaphor chain, in your writing, usually*

wears out after two or three extensions. After that, it takes away from your theme, and becomes as intrusive as rhyming. So come in with your metaphor, elaborate it once or twice to deepen the effect, and then go back to your original language.

But in conversation or written dialogue, metaphor elaboration can be the basis of great charm or great fun. Here's one example, when a European man is seated next to an American woman, and wants to become acquainted over the airline's dinner:

"I'm sorry," he said. *"I don't mean to intrude. But I do have a problem."*

"I don't understand," she said.

"I'm European. And I'd like to have my dinner now. But I can't, unless you do."

"I'm afraid that I ..."

"Don't know European customs. Of course. May I explain?"
She nodded weakly.

"You see," he went on, *"because you're sitting there, and I'm sitting here, we are, in a sense, having dinner together. For example,"* and he lifted his plastic fork, *"there's simply no way I could raise this rather cheap utensil to my mouth, without noticing that you are not raising your rather cheap utensil to your mouth."*

She smiled.

"Good," he said. *"You're beginning to understand the delicacy of the situation. Now, think deeply about this for a moment. Are you really prepared to let me starve? Are you, shall we say, prepared to take the responsibility for having the airline carry this oversized body off the plane, when, just as easily, you could have allowed it to propel itself off under its own power?"*

Her smile grew broader. *"What in the world do you do?"* she asked.

"If it's a noble profession, will you feed me?"

"Yes. Alright. I give in."

"Then I'm afraid I really will starve." ...

What has this man done to be so charming and give his new acquaintance so much fun? He has set up a metaphorical universe, and persuaded her to come into it with him. It is a universe where having an isolated dinner is a *problem,* where a fork is a *cheap utensil,* where not eating is *starving,* where not having eaten is *being carried off the plane,* and where being fed depends on *pursuing a noble profession.*

He has spoken to her in the form of a metaphor chain. What would have been otherwise everyday and banal, is now filled with smiles, intrigues, and possible romance.

He has broken through her reserve by using unfinished statements *(I have a problem ... You don't know European customs ... Are you prepared to let me starve),* which we'll call *hooks,* and the out-of-the-ordinary.

They meet, they fall in love, and they marry ... all through the power of a metaphor chain.

8.   *Pump power into a word by putting it next to another that doesn't "belong" next to it.*

As we saw before, metaphor lets you place two universes of meaning right next to each other, by placing two words that participate in those universes right next to each other.

These two words, abutting each other, are many times more powerful than they would be separated. But this kind of 1 + 1 = 4 power is not just limited to metaphor.

Great power can come from abutting any two words that are not expected to share the same meaning, or that change each other's meaning in startling ways.

Again, this is the kind of power that poetry calls on, time after time. For example, *the enslaved God,* or *the cruel charity.* Each of the descriptive words here seems, at first glance, to contradict the actor words they flesh out.

But, again, the threat of contradiction causes your reader to pause and think. What he knew before he read the sentence has proved inadequate to understand it. Thus, he must look backward or forward in your words to find the answer.

Again, you see that your communication has two basic goals: to let your reader understand, and to make him think.

9.   *First get the idea down. Then sharpen it.*

As you write, one idea will lead to another. Sometimes they will come so fast that you will have to jot them down in a personal shorthand, to get them all down.

Don't worry about punch at this stage. Image, here, is being translated into words, and you have to complete that translation before you can think about style.

Then, when the idea chain has played itself out, go back over the sentences, one by one, and sharpen them. Your first job was to find out what you could say. Now you're ready to see how to say it best. Here is how you do this:

Cut where you can. If a word is not absolutely necessary, get rid of it. If it is the same as another word very close to it, get rid of one of them. If it telegraphs your end-of-sentence punch, drop it.

Take this first-draft example:

"The easier it is to use, the more often it will be used."

Here, *used* is used twice. You want to save it for the end, so cut it out of the front.

"The easier it is, the more often it will be used."

But *more often* repeats the same image in two words. Get rid of the second:

"The easier it is, the more it will be used."

Good. But could it be sharper, if the parallelism were strengthened? If both images had the same number of words? If the identity words in both phrases *(is* and *was)* took place at the same time? Try it:

"The easier it is, the more it's used."

Also good. Both this, and the one before, are acceptable. Your feeling for style – and for the surrounding context – will let you choose among them.

Remember, short is most often strong. You are really writing images, and you need to clothe them in just enough words that your reader can duplicate them.

Or, even better, in information writing, your words should be like shop windows. Your reader should be able to look right through them, and see your images inside.

10. *Help your reader remember.* First, you help him form a set of duplicate images to your own. Then you help him retain those images for a lifetime.

To do this, you use the memory devices that have worked for thousands of years. They are:

Punch. You remember best what moves you. What startles you, surprises you, threatens you, compels you to think, and gives you the white light of eventual understanding that we call insight.

Echo. Words that sound the same are stored the same. You want her to remember the image, but it doesn't hurt if she also remembers the words that call it up. If these words alliterate, the front-sounds serve as hooks for her to pull words and images up later. And once she has the hook in, she can pull up the entire kettle of fish. (Ouch!)

Metaphor. Make abstract thoughts easy with visual metaphors. Easy to learn, and easy to remember. That way, she has two brain circuits to rely on when she needs the information again. She can pull it up logically, or she can pull it up visually.

Parallelism. Like is remembered easier than unlike. Again, this is structure-echo. If he remembers one parallel clause, he's got a line to the other.

Steps in the ladder. For example, tell her there are *five* parts to this section. That *five* is a reminder, as well as a road sign. Later, when she needs them all, she'll know how many she has to look for.

Markings. Tell him what he has to remember in detail, and what he has to remember in less detail, and what he can forget. Much of your writing simply serves as preparation for your main points. Once he's understood them, he can forget that preparation. So make the preparation Information, and the main points Impact. And repeat the main points. And point out that they are indeed the main points.

11. *Borrow Truth.* Some complicated – or unfamiliar – ideas can be much better understood if you equate them with simpler ideas that work the same way. For example:

"Running a country is like running a marriage. You can't build it on lies."

How was this sentence built? On two mechanisms: Like, and last image.

The *like* mechanism lets you equate something new with something old. Something difficult with something easy. An unfamiliar definition of running a country with an almost too-familiar definition of running a marriage.

How do you do this? By letting your reader feed back the self-evident truth from *marriage,* and extending it to *country.*

But that truth is only evident when she reaches the last word. Then she uses it to construct her *unstated sentence:* *"You can't run a country on lies any more than you can run a marriage on lies."*

So punch here – like punch everywhere – depends on the unstated sentence. You never say that sentence, but you make sure that your reader has to think it.

Once he does, he experiences two simultaneous emotions – surprise and truth. He *feels* surprised, and he *feels* that what you're saying is true. Both are strong, biologically-based feelings. And when he feels both of them at the same time, he's blown away.

Surprise doubles the power of truth. Why? Because it strips away the defenses that truth so often encounters. We don't know where the punch is coming from, and so we have no defense against it.

So, first, borrow a simple truth to introduce a complex one. And then, if that truth is also hard to swallow, sweeten it with the surprise that end-of-sentence, feedback and implication make possible.

12. *The sentence-expanding clause, to express more complex ideas.*

In business, science, and other abstract fields, you will deal with unified thoughts that embrace several interdependent relationships. To break such thoughts up into individual sentences does not do them justice. So you use sentence-expanders to retain clarity within such length.

Here is an example taken from this chapter:

In our everyday use of language, synonyms are invaluable, because they allow you to express the same image, over and over again, in different words.

There are two main parts to this sentence: *In our everyday use of language, synonyms are invaluable,* and *because they allow you ...* The first part could stand by itself as a complete sentence. But you want to put into it the reason *why* they're invaluable. So you use *because* as a sentence-expander, and then you give that reason.

The word *because,* of course, says, "Here is the cause." It therefore allows you to tack one full sentence onto another, so you have an expanded sentence.

Notice that *because* allows you to link the two sentences together like the two passenger cars of a train. The first sentence, *In our everyday language, synonyms are invaluable,* is complete and uninterrupted. Nothing blocks the translation of its two images. Your reader has them vividly in her mind before she goes on to the *because* sentence that follows.

The key to success here is uninterruptedness. Yes, you can have immediately understandable sentences with several clauses, but they must be uninterrupted sentences. Each of the clauses must respect the integrity – the image-wholeness – of every other.

The sentence can be complex and interrelated, as long as each of the phrases within it can be converted into images as soon as they are encountered. But when image-conversion is blocked, the sentence must be rewritten.

Tacking-on with immediate understanding can be done at the sentence beginning, as well as its end. Can it be done in the middle? Yes, if the old sentence – which is going to be used as a part of the new sentence – is completed before you add on the new part. Or if you set off that new mid-sentence by vivid punctuation marks, such as dashes, and if you limit that mid-sentence to less than two lines, so that your reader can see both the start of the first sentence-part and its continuation over the mid-sentence.

I've written Section 12 in a more complex style than I've used in the rest of the book. Both the sentences and the paragraphs are longer. Yet I hope I've retained the immediate understanding throughout.

Short or long – one-part, two-part or multi-part – all are a matter of style and personal preference. Within these few rules, there are worlds of opportunity.

13. *Hooks. That keep your reader reading.* A hook is a verbal device that you put into your discourse to draw your reader into it, and keep him from escaping from it.

Let's go back to our man on the airplane in Section 7. He had a simple goal: To *hook* the lovely woman next to him into a romantic conversation. Since she was quite beautiful, she had probably swum past a thousand similar hooks. How could he bait this one so she couldn't get away?

If he'd said, *"What's your name?"* for example, he would have gotten brushed off, and the reader would have left your story. So he had to say something no one had said to her before.

That something was:

"I'm sorry," he said. *"I don't mean to intrude. But I do have a problem."*

"I don't understand," she said.

"I'm European. And I'd like to have my dinner now. But I can't, unless you do."

Let's pick out the hooks from his two sentences. They are:

... sorry ... won't intrude ... problem ... European ... like to have dinner, but can't unless you do.

Notice that these words establish the correct distance away from "intruding" upon her privacy. Since he is so correct, he assumes she will be correct too, and he's right. But then, from this "correct" distance, he begins to draw her in.

What he tells her then is a series of *incomplete* sentences. He says he has a problem, but he doesn't say what that problem is. That he's European, but not what being European means in this situation. That she's keeping him from his dinner, but not how she's doing this.

After each of these sentences, she has to listen on, to discover the thought that completes it. Each is melodramatic, and charming, enough to make her want to keep listening. She is hooked by the mystery and charm of the verbal universe he is building for her.

His hooks, like all hooks, depend on *incompleteness.* They therefore seem to deliberately reverse one of our basic rules: *Make every image complete when your listener first hears it.*

But look at them again. They are all complete enough to be understood, but they are understood as questions. When, for example, he says, *"I have a problem,"* she understands that he has it, but she asks herself what it is.

So, just as *punch relies on an unstated sentence,* so a *hook relies on an unstated question.* A hook, therefore, is a sentence that contains an unstated question. And which therefore impels your reader to *Feed Forward* to answer it.

Advertising copywriters use hooks all the time in their headlines. Think of *"Do you make these mistakes in English?"* ... *"Doctors' Amazing Secret Home Remedies"* ... or even *"Free!"* They're all hooks, and the more compelling the questions they raise, the more readers will venture into the ad to get their answers.

Where do you place your hooks, and how do you build

the most power into them? First, at the beginning of your discourse and your sentence. The first hook there is the incomplete Connecting Word – *If, When, Because, If ever, By the way, And then, Is this,* etc.

Next, the warning: *Vital Note, Beware, Be careful of, Don't,* etc.

Next, make the usual *unusual.* For example, go beyond our shrewd friend on the plane. Say, *"I have a heart-rending problem."* Or, *"There is a hidden contradiction in what you say."* Or, *"Do you know who John was seen with at two o'clock last night?"*

Listen to gossips. Read their columns in the daily paper. Study their leads. Jot down the hooks in them.

Realize that life is a series of opportunities for headlines. Read ads, not for their promises, but for their seductors.

Start each discourse with a hook. Then start each chapter with one. Then start each paragraph with one. Insert them more and more throughout your writing, until they become intrusive. And then cut out those that call attention to themselves, and not to what's coming next.

Then place them at the end. There, they're often called "cliff hangers." Every chapter should end with one. Here are some examples:

"But the most pathetic results are still to come."

"The next chapter will be devoted to some of the most devastating of these errors."

"She had to fix her face, and think about what little lies to tell Arlene."

"The crusade was failing. Time was running out. He was being driven into a corner again. And this time it might be a corner from which he would never escape."

Notice the words that transform an ordinary statement into a hook: *Some of the, what (little lies), who (he was seen with), a (problem), it might be a,* etc. All of them are general. Therefore, they force the reader to look ahead to fill in the details.

Remember – sentences that contain unstated questions. That force your reader to Feed Forward to answer them.

They get your words read.

14.   *Picture yourself debating.* You do it all the time, in your fantasies of what you should have said in the argument you've just lost. Now do it to win the argument in advance.

We all think of brilliant retorts an hour after we've left an argument. We write "scripts" of what we should have said, and what they'd say then, and how we'd go on to devastate their position.

These scripts, of course, are edited. We go over and over again what we should have said, until we have it just right. And we go over and over again what they would say, so they set us up for our final deadly thrust.

We play both sides of the debate. We sharpen our role, and their role, until it becomes, practically speaking, like theater. We do this all the time, but right now it's just fantasy, and we don't put this "automatic editing" tool to work for us.

Now use it deliberately. When you first write, just write. But when you edit, debate.

Check each pivotal point. Imagine your reader's reaction. Make her hostile. See if she, in your mind, can tear your logic apart. If she can, eliminate the weak point. Then let her have another shot at it.

Let her strengthen, strengthen, strengthen your position. And then take every way you can imagine her setting up your most powerful punches, and build those into Feed-Back sentences.

Give her different roles to play. Let her be a series of experts on what you're talking about. If you're discussing the plight of the poor, for example, let her be first a social worker, then the pastor who shelters the poor, then a conservative who attacks any government support, then the most articulate of the poor, etc.

As you give her roles, you'll find that, not only does she play her characters more and more vividly, but that you phrase your replies more and more powerfully.

15. *The beginning and the end.* There's where the hooks are, and there's where the punch is. Therefore, become beginning-conscious, and end-conscious. Jot down your first thoughts as they come to you, but edit them by checking every beginning and every end.

Remember, they'll be remembered, and the middles will largely be forgotten. They form the outlines of the images you're transmitting. And as long as your reader remembers the outlines, he has your thought actively influencing his brain.

16. *Your words should be transparent.* Your reader should be able to look right through them, and see the images beneath.

Think of the words as the wires, and the images as the electricity. The words deliver the effects. Then those words can be forgotten, and be replaced by their equivalents.

For you to call attention to the words is calling attention to the wires. When your reader says, "Isn't that well phrased," he's lost the image in the words. He may remember one or two of those words, but not what they said. He remembers you as a "good writer," but not as a source for his ideas.

Therefore, write powerfully, and not prettily. If you hear compliments on your style, and not on your ideas, change the style. Brilliance is neither showing off nor pretension. It is getting the communication job done.

Words disappear. Thoughts endure, and change the future.

Practice these techniques whenever you have the chance, either in your writing or in your speech. With each minor success, they become easier and easier, stronger and stronger, more and more memorable.

Who knows? Perhaps the next edition of this book – or of many other books – may contain *your* next unforgettable line.

Good searching. Good speaking. Good writing. Good luck.

– Eugene M. Schwartz